# LIVE TRUE

## A Mindfulness Guide to Authenticity

**Praise for Ora Nadrich and**

# *Live True*

"Ora Nadrich is one of my favorite wise women. Her teaching, her understanding, her love have all touched my life profoundly. The world is a better place because she casts her light upon it."

**—Marianne Williamson**
#1 *New York Times* bestselling author of
*A Return to Love*

"Living from our authentic core, we are able to create a more fulfilling and successful life for ourselves. Ora's unique strategy of intentional authenticity liberates the reader from mental and emotional baggage. Live True draws us into the current of our highest potential, greatest healing, and deepest love."

**—Jack Canfield**
Coauthor of the #1 *New York Times* bestselling
*Chicken Soup for the Soul®* series and *The Success Principles:
How to Get from Where You Are to Where You Want to Be*™

"Ora Nadrich is a skillful, compassionate Mindfulness teacher and a beautiful human being. I am blessed to have her as a friend."

**—Judith Orloff, MD**
*New York Times* bestselling author of
*The Empath's Survival Guide*

"This lovely book is a treasure trove of spiritual delights, offering words of wisdom and simple truths to help drop us down to a more present and balanced perspective. Keep it by your bedside and read it each day before getting out of bed. Or place it on your desk to offer respite in the midst of your daily routines. Gifted teacher, Ora Nadrich has provided practices to help us live with a greater sense of sweetness, goodness and love."

**—Katherine Woodward Thomas**
*New York Times* bestselling author of *Calling in "The One"* and *Conscious Uncoupling*

"With elegant simplicity, *Live True* beckons us to explore new depths within ourselves. Ora Nadrich helps us redefine what it means to live mindfully in a way that is authentic, honest, and real. These pages are filled with beauty and wisdom."

**—Marci Shimoff**
#1 *New York Times* bestselling author of *Happy for No Reason* and *Chicken Soup for the Woman's Soul*

"Ora's message of authenticity will resonate with readers on many levels. She is a master at weaving through the clutter of our modern minds and helping us find our healing. Her work is a wonderful gift to us all."

**—David Kessler**
Coauthor of *New York Times* bestsellers *You Can Heal Your Heart* and *On Grief and Grieving*

"Ora speaks to the most relevant psychological and spiritual themes of today, and brings a new facet to the modern application of timeless truth. She delivers her transmission through poetry, simple wisdom, and meditation. Her book *Live True* is a personal spirit guide for a self-led journey, an active exploration of the meaning of one's life."

**—Benjamin W. Decker**
Author of *Practical Meditation for Beginners*

"Ora Nadrich's compelling invitation to drop into the "Eternal Now" could not be more timely or more necessary. Live True should be required reading for all human beings."

**—Peter Rader**
Author of *Playing to the Gods* and Producer of *Awake: The Life of Yogananda*

"*Live True* is a relevant and important book to read in today's times. Ora, once again, has done a marvelous job in empowering the human spirit through her inspiring writing and helpful meditation guidance. Being authentic is the highest form of courage, and this book is a timely reminder of it. I highly recommend it!"

**—Chandresh Bhardwaj**
Author of *Break the Norms: Questioning Everything You Think You Know About God and Truth, Life and Death, Love and Sex*

# LIVE TRUE

## A Mindfulness Guide to Authenticity

### ORA NADRICH

THE INSTITUTE FOR
IFTT
PRESS
TRANSFORMATIONAL THINKING

Published in Los Angeles, California, by The IFTT Press. The IFTT Press is a trademark of The Institute For Transformational Thinking, LLC.
IFTTPress.org

Live True
A Mindfulness Guide to Authenticity
© 2019 Ora Nadrich

ISBN: 978-0-578-41596-3 (Hardcover edition)
ISBN: 978-0-578-43210-6 (Paperback edition)
ISBN: 978-0-578-43211-3 (Ebook edition)

Library of Congress Control Number: 2018913554

Published 2019
Cover embellishments & design by Dmitriy Khanzhin
Cover photo by Simon Migaj
Edited by Kathleen Felesina

The Institute For Transformational Thinking is an international academy offering certifications in Thought Coaching, Meditation, and more. The IFTT provides an immersive experience through online courses, retreats, webinars, blogs, and an online directory of IFTT certified professionals.
TheIFTT.org

## TRANSFORMATIONAL
# THINKING

Transformational Thinking is a monthly digital publication provided by The IFTT.
TransformationalThinkingMonthly.com

Transformational Schools provides training in Mindfulness for teachers, faculty, students and parents.
TransformationalSchools.org

# CONTENTS

*For Esther*

"I shan't be lonely now. I was lonely; I was afraid. But the emptiness and the darkness are gone; when I turn back into myself now I'm like a child going at night into a room where there's always a light."

—Edith Wharton

Eternal gratitude for my beloved family; Jeff, Jake and Ben. You fill my heart daily with pure joy.

# Foreword
## by Dr. Ronald Alexander

Ora has written a wonderful and clear guide, utilizing Mindfulness and meditation as a backdrop to assist us in discovering who we are at our core level of integrity and authenticity. As Buddha beings, we learn to pay attention to each and every moment with a fresh lens of awareness; a teaching brought forth by the Buddha 2400 years ago to assist us as a map to discover learning, and to navigate the territory of the self.

These writings and teachings were brought forth shortly after the death of Ora's sister, Esther, which had such a profound impact on her, it caused Ora to look deeper into her own soul to look upon the essence of who we really are, and by opening the door of inner exploration, we discover the truth of our being even more.

As a guide, these writings invite the reader to gently begin engaging further into the self, soul and psyche, and undertake the transformational journey to look inward to who and what we really are, and connect to our core essence in the moment. As a call to one's heart and soul, Ora invites the reader to explore themselves more thoroughly, and not be afraid to meet their most true, authentic self. It's a captivating invitation to awaken to the highest level of soulful enlightenment and self-realization.

In any journey of awakening, we must go down to the deepest level of our being, where what you will discover there is so much richer and deeply textured than what you can observe on the surface of self-knowledge. It is these spiritual core findings, which Ora has written about, that help direct us towards a more meaningful, and more personal realization of ourselves.

As a map of self-realization in each and every chapter, there are meditative jewels and tools to guide you to wake up from hiding your true inner "Buddha Nature." This is very timely since we are facing many challenges in these times of spiritual, political and cultural change. It is these very challenges that require us to be our most authentic self, right here and now. We can, and must become more aware of our true, benevolent nature so that we can spread this important message that is needed more than any time in all of history. Ora highly advocates self-awareness, and suggests with enthusiasm that we must, and can become the fully realized beings that reside hidden in the depths of our inner being, so that we can fulfill our destinies with clear purpose and intention.

It is through the practice of Mindfulness, as Ora writes about, that you become more cognizant of when you lose awareness of yourself and your environment, and are taught through her guidance, how to return with a new-found presence again and again to the present moment, which is a very needed and most powerful skill to remain conscious and awake.

Mindfulness, coupled with authenticity, teaches us that this new-found awareness of our most true self, keeps us fully present with a deeper and more clear understanding of who we are, and our purpose in this life. It helps us let go of suffering more readily, and awaken to an inner peace of authentic spiritual development. Authenticity, Ora feels, is more important than ever as a prescription for peace, happiness and fulfillment, and living your truth fills that prescription.

In short, Ora distills both Mindfulness and authenticity, and combines them so seamlessly that we can practice the power and efficacy of her effective Mindfulness/Authenticity philosophy with comfort and ease. It is presented to us in a brisk, informative, and easy to understand narrative; punctuated with tailored meditations, relatable anecdotes, and other useful supplementary information to be used in our day-to-day lives. This guide teaches you how to show up in all of the moments of your life, as present and as real as you can be.

Ora's two decades of training and practice as both a Life Coach and certified Mindfulness meditation instructor is synthesized into a compelling work of prescriptive non-fiction that is designed to inform, inspire and create a call to action for readers to take charge and change their lives. Rise up and wake up to the call of "living in the present moment with truth and authenticity", as the title suggests. This book will kindle and fire a deep desire and passion in you to "be here now", and to do the here and now as your most real, authentic self.

Ronald Alexander, Ph.D.
Author, *Wise Mind / Open Mind*
Founder, OpenMind Training Institute

# Introduction

*Your vision will become clear only when you can look
into your own heart. Who looks outside, dreams;
who looks inside, awakes.*
*—Carl Jung*

This moment you are in right now—the Present Moment—
is the most important moment there is. You are alive in it,
and it is uniquely yours. It is unlike any other moment you
have ever had, or will have again. Yesterday has come and
gone, tomorrow is not here yet. It is this present moment
that matters the most, and if we value the moments of our
lives, we will want to make the most of each one, and not let
any moment go by without having lived it as truthfully and
authentically as we can.

But what does it mean to live "Authentically"?

The definition of authentic is "genuine" and "real"; or, in other words, the combination of all your true qualities and characteristics. However, I like to describe authentic as "living your truth in the present moment." I know, it's easy to want to hide or conceal certain aspects of ourselves we may not love, but once we start to hide our realness and who we really are, it can slip away from us to the point that we are living dishonestly to our true nature, and why would we want to do that?

*Fear, insecurity, doubt.*

Those are some of the reasons that strip us of our true nature. And before we know it, we are not living our truth in the present moment, or any of the moments of our lives if we are not aware of the traps of our mind, which are the lies we tell ourselves that keep us stuck in self-deception.

Mindfulness, which is living in the present moment with total awareness, keeps us honest, and true to who we are. It reminds us when we slip out of the moment of authenticity, and try and hide or replace it with a false belief of ourselves, and that's what we'll be exploring in this book.

But it won't stop there. I will direct you to the home of your authenticity, which is the depths of your inner being. That is where you will find your wholeness, and feel most accepting and complete. The inner-self is the dwelling place of our authenticity, but too often we stray from our authentic wholeness, and it can become fragmented or even broken. I will show you through a variety of meditations in each chapter, how to return back to, and connect with your inner-self, so you can live your authentic wholeness in all that you do.

To live authentically means being connected—in a mindful way—to all aspects of ourselves, and the core values we adhere to and live by. Mindfulness and authenticity are inexorably linked—you cannot be effectively mindful without being authentic. And Mindfulness is extremely important: it helps us not forget our true nature. It keeps us present and aware. If we feel an impulse to be inauthentic, it reminds us immediately that falseness of any kind feels wrong with every fiber of our being.

It's been said that when the Buddha became enlightened, he realized that all human beings have the same nature and potential for enlightenment. This is called "Buddha nature."

What we know about Siddhartha Gautama, which in Sanskrit means, "enlightened one" and who became a Buddha, is that he set out to find the truth of human existence, and the only way he knew how to find it was by taking the inner journey, and going deep within himself. And deep he went. So much so that he found what he was looking for: the knowing that desire and attachment are at the root of our unhappiness, and until we transcend what perpetuates our suffering, we will remain at the effect of our longings, which will keep us unconscious, destined to relive our problems.

Buddha knew that the only way we can truly know who we are is to look within, and go beyond the illusions of what we tell ourselves and believe. That is where we will find our "true nature", the *authentic self*, and from there, we can live each day aspiring to become more conscious by peeling away the layers of who we are not; the inauthentic self.

We have a long way to go before we can transcend desire and attachment. But by knowing ourselves better, and determining who we authentically are, we can stay on the path of awareness, rather than continue our suffering through ignorance.

In order to achieve this, we must be willing to be present, and meet the moments of our lives with openness and acceptance. We cannot become aware of the authentic self if we are not surrendered to who we are in the moment, and always looking to the past or the future to define us, which is usually where we spend the most time in our heads. Mindfulness, this very moment of "now," is the gateway to self-realization, and is what teaches us how to be more cognizant of our "aliveness" so we can face whatever we are experiencing consciously.

***Without being present, we cannot be fully aware, and without being fully aware, we remain unconscious.***

This is what Buddha helped us understand through his own enlightenment. He showed us the "way" to finding our true selves, which is to look inside, and what we will find there may surprise us more than we can imagine. Yes, there is suffering in our hearts, but there is also reason to feel tremendous joy too. But to find true happiness, we must look beyond our identity, our desires, and our attachments, just as Buddha looked beyond being a royal prince born into wealth. He knew that material wealth does not guarantee happiness, and that we are much more than who we think we are and what we have.

We are Buddha's waiting to awaken. Take this journey with me to discover your most authentic self, and the truth of who you are in the present moment. The moments of our lives are meant to rouse us from our unconsciousness. We mustn't be foolish and rush through them, but instead value and savor them, for they hold the answers for our full awakening.

*Let us awaken now!*

*Be congruent, be authentic, be your true self.*
*—Mahatma Gandhi*


*We need enlightenment, not just individually, but collectively to save the planet. We need to awaken ourselves. We need to practice mindfulness if we want to have a future, if we want to save ourselves, and the planet.*
*—Thich Nhat Hanh*

# PART I

## TIME

*I wasted time, and now doth time waste me.*
*—William Shakespeare*

# CHAPTER 1

# Now

*Past and future are in the mind only—I am now.*
*—Sri Nissergadatta Maharaj*

Y ou are exactly where you need to be. Where you find yourself is where you have taken yourself by choice, and it is here—in this moment—that you will learn what it has to show or teach you, especially if you are facing something difficult or painful.

We don't usually think of the moments of our life as an opportunity to learn something valuable about ourselves. Instead, we often take them for granted. **But each and every moment can be our greatest teachers**. If we let them slip away and waste them, they are gone, and the benefits to be gained, such as learning how we can change the things about ourselves we want to improve or strengthen, or how we can be more conscious in our relationships, which gives us the opportunity for greater awareness, are not fully realized.

But who are we to waste life's moments, or assume they should be wasted? Were we given them to only appreciate when they offer us joy and material luxuries, or to value only the good ones? On the contrary, moments—both good and bad—are not just experiences; they are more about the lessons that are hidden in them, *and those lessons are intended just for us.* All of them are good because they are ours. If we can accept them as true gifts, we will show up for them, and never turn our back on, or waste a single one again.

A moment gives us a brief period to be fully present, and be our most authentic self, before it completely vanishes like magic. Now you see it, now you don't. But this isn't a magic show. This is our life: it's very real, and very short. Moments will keep appearing, one after the other, until we inhale our very last breath. But unfortunately, we take many of those moments for granted, and waste them on negative, unproductive thoughts because we are not being true and authentic to ourselves.

Each moment of our lives deserves our attention, or else they will leave us, one by one, like a forlorn lover, never having been given the best of who we are. But which moments are we saving our personal best for? Why be withholding or stingy with a moment that gives us the air to breathe, instead of being thankful that we are alive for another moment?

4

The time we waste is the time we pray to be given when the end of life is near. We ask for more time, realizing that the moments diverted from living in the present are gone forever, wasted. That's why it's so important to love all the moments of your life, even the ones that seem unlovable. They might be hard to love because they've hurt you, disappointed you, or even felt like they abandoned you. Moments can break our hearts, especially the painful ones, and we can hate them and curse them and never want to see them again. But they can also bring us a baby, a liver transplant, a soul mate, or something as satisfying as a smile from a complete stranger. Sometimes the simplest moment is the richest. And it cost you absolutely nothing. It was free.

That's what moments are. They are 100% free. Moments are the gift that keeps on giving, and we don't have to pay a single penny for them. A moment doesn't need our money. It just wants us to be happy, and not to suffer. Even though it can be the messenger of bad news, we must not "kill the messenger". A moment is simply doing its job, and when it brings us pleasure and joy, and we're pleased with what it gives us, we can even say with satisfaction, "I got completely lost in the moment." But even a difficult or painful moment can leave us with a strength we never knew we had, or an awareness of how to move through our pain in a more tolerant, conscious way.

*But we mustn't forget that a moment is nothing more than time.* That's it. And it lives on with or without us. We borrow from its infinite supply.

But when we're not grateful for what time gives us, and wasteful of the moments it presents us, time doesn't care.

5

It marches on. Our life moments are less than a blink of an eye in time's continuum. It just gives us what we need like oxygen, and we decide what we want to do with it; either breathing from it fully with all of our being, or taking shallow unconscious breaths, half breathing into life, which is only being partly alive.

So, this is it. This is your moment to live it as you choose to. You can live it fully, mindfully and in gratitude, or you can live it wishing for another moment to be better, or top the one you're in. But what's going to be better than this moment *right now*? Happiness will continue to elude us if we are constantly longing for what "could be" rather than accepting "what is." All of the moments of your life are meant to be lived as if they are your last.

*This moment.* Live it as truthfully and authentically as you possibly can, and live it with love and acceptance. It will never return. Poof, it's gone....

# Meditation for Being in the Moment of "Now"

1.  Find a quiet place to sit.

2.  Close your eyes.

3.  Feel yourself where you are right now.

4.  Note the room: any sounds, thoughts, feelings, or bodily sensations. Simply observe them.

5.  Invite yourself to be present in your meditation.

6.  Tell yourself it's okay to let everything and everyone go.

7.  Put your focus and awareness onto your breath.

8.  Take a few deep breaths in and out.

9.  If your mind begins to wander at any time, bring your focus and awareness back to your breath, which will always bring you back to the present moment.

10. Say silently, "I am in this moment of now."

11. Say silently, "Now is all there is."

12. Say silently, "I accept this moment I am in."

13. You can repeat this to yourself as many times as you wish.

14. When you are ready slowly open your eyes.

15. Be aware that you are still in the moment of "now," and that there is no need to rush out of it.

16. *Take your time to transition out of your meditation.*

*(Note: The following "Note to self" is the essence of the lesson you've learned from each chapter, and can be used as a friendly reminder.)*

**Note to self:**

**Now is the most real moment there is
I live in the moment of now**

# CHAPTER 2

## This Magic Moment

*Magic is believing in yourself,*
*if you can do that, you can make anything happen.*
*—Johann Wolfgang von Goethe*

There are those moments in our lives that are just so good we can best describe them as magical. When they happen, we feel it with every fiber of our being. It's like our entire self is bubbling inside like a bottle of champagne that waits to be open, its cork shooting out so fast by the force of the bubbles. When that magic happens, we feel the amazing power of the life force within us, and we don't want it to stop, not even for a moment.

This is when life feels it's at its finest. Yet, when life gives us those types of incredible moments, ordinary ones just don't feel as good, and life can suddenly feel dull or boring, which can challenge our sense of well-being.

The truth is that all of the moments of our lives are magical because we are alive in them. Unfortunately, we don't always see it that way because we want *all* the moments of our lives to be magical, don't we? We want them to surprise and gift us, to awe and love us, pamper and spoil us, and tell us how good and lovable we are. When that stops happening we don't like it, and can even get angry. *How dare you moments of my life stop being magical? How dare you not elevate me to heights so high, I can forget my woes and troubles, and feel instead like I'm levitating right out of my body? You can't give that to me all the time? Well, if not, I'm going to make my own magic by elevating myself with money, or sex, or food, or drugs, or alcohol—any of those things that make me feel so good that I've got the magic with me 24/7.*

A magical moment reminds us of how magical life can be, but it doesn't mean its job is to entertain us, or inebriate us, or exalt us, or make us feel special all of the time. That's putting the burden onto something outside of ourselves. When the moments of our lives are simply ordinary, or even dull, we feel so robbed of magic we can barely stand it. And we wait for the magic to happen. *When is the magic going to begin? When is something wonderful or amazing going to happen for me? I need it, and I need it now.*

## The truth is:

### You are the magic.

### You are the high.

### You are the drug. You are wonderful.

### You are amazing.

### *You!*

You're probably looking around like this is about someone else. Someone who seems more amazing because they look amazing, and they act amazing and they have so many amazing things happen to them all of the time, and you don't. So, what does that mean? That they have more magic than you? That they got extra magic moments when they were being handed out by the magic Gods? No. Magic doesn't work that way. **Real magic comes from within.**

Yes, there's outside magic like sunsets, rainbows and eclipses, as well as many magical places and mystical lands. The world is full of magical places like the Taj Mahal, or the Grand Canyon, or the Sorcerer's Castle in Switzerland, and you can travel to see that kind of magic whenever you want to. But what do you do when you can't go to the magic, but want the magic to come to you?

That's when you turn to the magic within you. You sit quietly, breathe, and go within to the most magical place of all, yourself. This is the first step of practicing Mindfulness, a practice that will allow you to access "The Magic Within" whenever you desire.

Indeed, there's a lot of magic right there, deep within you, and it's magic like no other because it's *your* magic. There's magic in all of the crevices of your being. In the nooks and crannies of your soul. In your cells, your blood, and in each of your organs. That's right—your organs. It takes magic to pump your heart, and breathe in and out approximately 17,000-30,000 times a day. It takes magic to have a mind that can think whatever it wants and solve problems. It takes magic to have a body that knows exactly what to do to keep you healthy. It takes magic to be alive in this very moment, and each magical moment after this one.

But if you keep going out of the moment, thinking that another one will be better, you're escaping the magic, and magic isn't going to chase you. Magic doesn't want to work that hard. Magic wants you to be ready and receptive to it, and how can you be ready and receptive if you're running away, or hiding, or complaining? So stop. Stop all the commotion. Stop all the drama. Stop being spoiled. Stop being selfish. Stop being negative. Stop being ungrateful. Stop feeling sorry for yourself. Just stop all that.

Find your stillness. Find your acceptance. Find your gratitude. And most of all find you in the magic. You're there. You're the magic moment. Now let it happen and it will. Believe in yourself.

# *Magic Moment Meditation*

1.  Find a quiet place to sit.

2.  Close your eyes.

3.  Invite yourself to be present in your meditation.

4.  Note the room: any sounds, thoughts, feelings, or bodily sensations. Simply observe it.

5.  Tell yourself it's okay to let everything and everyone go.

6.  Release any tension you might be holding in your body.

7.  Put your focus and awareness onto your breath.

8.  Take a few deep breaths in and out.

9.  Say silently, "This moment is magical."

10. Say silently, "The magic is within me."

11. Say silently, "I am the magic."

12. Repeat this to yourself as many times as you wish.

13. When you are ready slowly open your eyes.

14. Be aware that you are still in the moment of "now," and that there is no need to rush out of it.

15. *Take your time to transition out of your meditation.*

## *Note to self:*

*Find my stillness*
*Find my acceptance*
*Find my gratitude*
*Find me in the magic*
*I am here*
*I am the magic*

# CHAPTER 3

# The Past

*Yesterday is gone. Tomorrow has not yet come.*
*We have only today. Let us begin.*
*— Mother Teresa*

You have lived the past already. It has come and gone—it's over. All that remains are your memories of it, or objects that you've kept from it. You cannot physically be in the past—it's impossible. And yet, we return to it again and again in our minds with thoughts and images, regrets, remembrances and what ifs. What we tell ourselves about our past remains present with us now, so the past will continue to exist in the present by our keeping it alive.

For most of us, our past contains some unpleasant or painful memories. As we know, that's part of life. It's how we've processed those painful experiences, however, and what we continue to tell ourselves about them that can make the biggest difference in how our past affects the present, and how much suffering we experience. That is, if we continue to tell ourselves negative things about our past, the negativity is what will remain.

Remember, an experience from the past has already been lived, and even though you can relive it in your mind, physically you can't because you are no longer in the past, or in the experience you once had. You experienced it, and now it's over. What needs to be done now is to change your thinking (or story around it), which will then change the intensity of the energy attached to it, which is being kept energized by you. Think of your experience as something attached to an electrical cord plugged into an outlet, which you can unplug at any time.

Are you ready to change what you think about a situation or experience you've had in your past? Are you ready to let go of something or someone that hurt you either mentally or physically? Maybe you've been abused, or violated in some way, and you can play it over and over again in your mind. You might even be feeling; "I can see and feel that horrible experience, as if it were just yesterday, and it's still very real for me."

Our experiences are very real for us because we lived them, and we know exactly what they felt like. That's why the painful ones don't stop being painful, even though they're over. The reason is those experiences are in our sense memory; meaning we can recall an experience through our senses, and by doing so, evoke an emotional reaction to it. That means we can smell what that experience smelled like, or hear the sounds we heard when we had that experience, or feel in a part of our body what we felt when we physically had that experience. It's like waking up to the smell of coffee in the morning—your sense memory processes that as a positive experience based on your memories of having it before and liking it, and so you start off the day in a great mood. The same goes for an unpleasant or painful experience, such as the sound of a person shouting at someone, which might make you recall a parent yelling at you when you were a child, causing you to presently feel anxious, which is an example of how a past experience can still trigger us in the present.

But we can replace those types of feelings and sensations with new thoughts, and a different story around it. This is the power of creating a new memory in its place, which becomes the ***memory in present time***. That doesn't mean that what's happened to you in your past is being treated as if it didn't happen or minimized, and what it did to you is being denied or diminished in any way. You're just processing it in a new way, and creating a different impression in its place.

You deserve to feel whatever you want to about an experience you've endured from your past. But by replacing what you tell yourself about what happened to you means that you don't have to keep reliving the unpleasantness or pain over and over again in your mind.

You don't have to suffer in the present like you suffered in the past, and be tormented by something that has already happened to you, unless you want to. It's a choice you can make, and once you do, you're putting the past where it belongs, in the past, which is defined as "gone by in time and no longer existing."

# *Memory in Present Time Meditation*

1. Find a quiet place to sit.

2. Close your eyes.

3. Invite yourself to be present in your meditation.

4. Note the room: any sounds, thoughts, feelings, or bodily sensations. Simply observe it.

5. Tell yourself it's okay to let everything and everyone go.

6. Release any tension you might be holding in your body.

7. Put your focus and awareness onto your breath.

8. Take a few deep breaths in and out.

9. If your mind begins to wander at any time, bring your focus and awareness back to your breath.

10. Think of an unpleasant time or experience from your past.

11. See yourself watching it like an observer or a witness, as if you were watching a play.

12. Think of yourself as the director of this memory-play, telling you and whoever is in it with you what to do, and change what you remember from your experience to something entirely different. You can be wearing whatever you want, doing whatever you want, and having whoever is in this memory-play with you doing exactly what you want them to be doing.

13. If anyone in this memory-play has an intention to hurt you, see yourself in control and in the power position, averting any conflict or harm.

14. If someone in your memory-play has hurt you emotionally, or you've hurt them, see yourself or them saying, "I'm sorry" or "I forgive you."

15. If someone in your memory-play is ill, tell them you surround them in healing light, and if they're dying, tell them that it's okay to leave this earth, and that you love them.

16. See yourself as strong and powerful, and imagine a bright white light surrounding you from head to toe.

17. Say silently, "I am more powerful than anyone or anything outside of myself."

18. Say silently, "Nothing or no one has a hold on me or my memory."

19. Say silently, "I am the creator of the thoughts and images I hold in my mind."

20. Say silently, "I am free of my past. I am at peace."

21. Slowly open your eyes.

22. *When you are ready transition out of your meditation.*

It's important to take back and reclaim our power from anything that has happened to us in our past that was unpleasant or painful, and the "Memory In Present Time Meditation" will help you do that if an uncomfortable memory starts to play over in your mind, and you find yourself feeling any sensations in your body from a past trauma. By putting that experience into a present context, you can reprocess and rewrite it as your empowered, authentic self, in spite of a difficult experience you have had, which will no longer have power over you. By practicing the "Memory In Present Time Meditation", you will be able to distance and desensitize yourself from an unpleasant memory, and choose instead to stay present, and not at the affect of it if it comes up for you. It's important to know that anything that has happened to us in the past does not define who we are in the present.

Allow yourself to feel fully embodied in present time. Acknowledge that you have created a new belief about whatever unpleasant thing happened to you in your past, and that if/when the memory of it returns, you know that **you are the creator of the thoughts and images you hold in your mind**, and can create a new, present memory in its place.

You are the director of your life movie, and can change, alter, enhance, and even erase an image, impression, scene, or scenario that serves no positive purpose for you to hold onto. Our memories create pictures in our minds, and we can change them, rearrange them, or delete them as we wish.

And remember, the present moment is the only moment you are alive in. You are no longer alive in a time called the past. It no longer exists, so therefore you cannot exist in it. This is your life movie happening right now. You are the star, director, writer, and producer.

When you call "action!" it all begins.

*Note to self:*

*The past no longer exists*
*What has happened to me doesn't define me*
*Who I was yesterday is not who I am today*

# CHAPTER 4

# The Present

*In rivers, the water that you touch is the last of what
has passed and the first of that which comes;
so with present time.*
—*Leonardo da Vinci*

As you are reading this, you are in the present moment. Can you be with it and accept it, or do you want to be somewhere else? If you do, ask yourself where would you rather be than in this very moment, and why?

Now that you've answered that, bring your awareness back to this moment because it's a different moment than the one before it. Can you see how seamlessly one moment moves into another? And when we move with it without resistance, that seamlessness becomes what we experience, and it feels smooth and weightless.

Most of the time, however, we can feel anything but weightless in a moment, especially if it's one that's challenging, difficult, daunting or intimidating, or makes us feel uncertain, insecure, or angry. We feel its heaviness, and we immediately constrict. But if we allow ourselves to open to it with acceptance, our resistance begins to dissolve, and we feel a lightness of being. We can now tell ourselves; "I can handle this moment. There is nothing for me to fear."

This is when we can direct the moment, meaning we can navigate it with neutrality because we are no longer constricting or reacting to the moment we're in, but instead allowing for it "to be". Being in the present with total awareness allows us to *observe* it so that we can watch its unfolding as if we were watching the sun rise or set. We don't tell the sun how to do what it knows to do so brilliantly, we simply watch, and we experience what we're seeing with acceptance.

Being in the moment as an observer does not mean that we are detached from it. It means that we are in the moment, but we don't have to be affected by it with unawareness.

When we're unaware of ourselves in a moment, it's easy to respond or react to what's going on unconsciously. That is why we say and do things impulsively, and wish we hadn't. We act without an awareness of being in the moment mindfully. We are not being an observer, and taking in the entire breadth of a moment, which can have many layers to it, many messages, many meanings, not to mention many emotional triggers that we need to be mindful of. When we bypass observing and go into reacting, we are unable to think clearly because our awareness is fuzzy and unfocused and we are easily triggered.

By being present and aware in a moment, we are cognizant of whatever is occurring; be it pleasant or difficult, and our awareness of it tells us exactly what to do. It literally guides us step by step in the most helpful and necessary way.

This is consciousness working. We are fully awake and aware of our surroundings and everything we're experiencing. You cannot know what to do in a moment that is difficult if you are not awake and aware in it. By being fully awake and aware in a moment, we can decide how we want to be in it, and what we want to do with it.

Remember, if you stay open in a moment, you can receive what it has to give you, but if you resist it or constrict, the moment cannot penetrate you, and it will pass you by.

You may think, "I have no problem with a moment passing me by if it's difficult or painful. As a matter of fact, I'd prefer that it move quickly so I can move through it as fast as possible." It's completely understandable that we want the unpleasant moments of our life to move by quickly, and would prefer if they never even came around at all.

The first of the Four Noble Truths, which are Buddha's teachings, is "suffering exists", but that doesn't mean we have to suffer more than we need to by reacting to it. By having an awareness of our suffering, we can move through it better by understanding it. Opening up to the suffering, instead of resisting it, helps us ease into it and grow from it, and as I mentioned, it can have a very valuable lesson for us to learn.

But if we avoid those opportunities, the moments of our lives will be greatly diminished by our unwillingness to work with, and appreciate, all of life's moments, including the painful ones. A single moment can have one of the most important lessons of our life in it, which can be the very thing we need to know and understand about ourselves, another person, or the situation we find ourselves in. If we rush through it without reflecting or observing, we are in danger of missing what might be a valuable lesson. Indeed, by being open to these moments, we can awaken even more to who we really are.

Do you wish to awaken more, or would you prefer to be half asleep, mired in unawareness?

Ask yourself: Do you want to be present? Do you want to live your life in the moment that exists right now, fully aware and awake? Or do you prefer to be in a moment that no longer exists, like the past, or a moment that has not yet come, the future?

This present moment is the moment that matters the most because you are in it, and, as I said, if you value being alive, then you value the moment you are most alive in, which is right now. It can be magical, amazing, mediocre, dull, boring, painful, or unbearable. It's whatever it is; you're the one in it, and you're the only one that can navigate it. How do you want to guide it? How do you want to handle it? How do you want to know it? How do you want to move through it?

Do you want the moments of your life to move seamlessly from one to the next, or do you want them to be jarring and jagged and disruptive? You can choose.

The moments of your life can feel like you're on a bumpy ride, bopping up and down like a rag doll. Or you can choose to see yourself as a surfer, riding each wave with grace and composure. Again, by easing into a moment, you morph into it, and then more easily transform it.

Think of yourself as liquid and malleable, able to take the shape of something that is hard or sharp, and by your presence in it, can soften it and make it more pleasant or palatable. You are a transformer, and can change anything by believing you can.

By keeping yourself open, you are able to be a larger container for whatever it is you are experiencing, and bring the moment into the magnificence of your being. As Walt Whitman said; "I am large, I contain multitudes." You can handle much more than you may think you can, and the moments of your life await your multitudinous ability. But you must be present. You must be aware. And you must be here. Exactly where you are right this very moment. There is nowhere else to be.

# Meditation for Present Moment Awareness

1. Sit somewhere quiet.

2. Close your eyes.

3. Be aware of any sounds, thoughts, feelings, or sensations in your body. Simply observe them.

4. Put your awareness and focus on your breath.

5. Take a few deep breaths in and out.

6. Say silently, "I am alive in this moment."

7. Say silently, "I am present in this moment."

8. Say silently, "I can handle this moment."

9. Say silently, "This moment is enough."

10. Locate a place in your body that feels centering or grounding—it could be your belly, heart, third eye; the place between your brow, or the base of your spine. Think of it as your power point or anchor.

11. Put the palm of your hand or fingertips on that place and feel it rising and falling with your breath.

12. Imagine that there is no separation between you and your breath, and that you and it are one organism breathing together.

13. Allow yourself to feel the oneness of you and your breath, spending as much time as you want in the vastness of this place, as if you are floating in an ocean that is carrying you gently along.

14. When you are ready, bring your awareness back to your body, acknowledging yourself sitting in mediation.

15. Slowly open your eyes.

16. *Take as much time as you need to transition out of your meditation.*

You can recreate this sensation of oneness, which is feeling complete, content, unified, or whole whether you are in a meditation or not.

When you find yourself feeling that you are not fully present, or beginning to react to whatever you're experiencing in a moment, put your focus and awareness on your breath. Remember your non-separation from it.

You can also either visualize your inner power point or anchor, like your belly or heart, or put your hand on it, and feel it rising and falling with each breath. This action will always return you to the present moment with more awareness. By doing this with consistency, you will find that you catch yourself more quickly when you're about to slip out of the present moment, and bring yourself right back to it with more ease. And know that when you go in and out of a moment with acceptance and non-judgment, you are opening up to it without resistance, and will experience the seamlessness of a moment moving into another.

### *You are the surfer. Ease into the wave.*

Another way to bring yourself back into the present moment when your mind begins to wander is to focus on something that pleases or interests you. Look around where you are and stop at the first thing that catches your eye. It could be a piece of art, or a vase filled with flowers. Look at the design or patterns on a rug. Maybe it's a person or an animal. If it's a person, watch their mannerisms. Do they look happy or sad? Do they look distracted and out of the moment? If it's an animal, what are they doing? You can observe a cat licking itself, and how fastidious it is in cleaning between each of its toes. If you're outside, notice a tree. What do its roots look like? Are its flowers in bloom? Is there fruit hanging from it? Are there birds on the branches? Are they chirping or hopping around? Or you can do something as simple as look up at the sky and follow a cloud. That's one of my favorite things to look at because it always reminds me that nothing is permanent, and things are always moving.

An everyday Mindfulness exercise to do, which is another one of my personal favorites, is be aware of what you see when you're stopped at a red light, which is a very useful time to practice observing. Look at the people that are crossing the street. It could be a woman strolling her baby, or a man in a suit, holding a cup of coffee and a briefcase, looking hurried. Maybe it's a homeless person, or a couple holding hands. You can also practice this if you use public transportation like subways or trains, and also on a plane flight. *Be not only aware of what you see, but also aware of what thoughts come to your mind.* Are you being judgmental, or are you feeling kindness or compassion?

***There is so much for us to take in and observe, and in our observations we are completely in the moment by how aware we are of the very thing we are looking at.***

I call this **life gazing**, and when we take the time to simply look around us, we can see so much more than when we're busy thinking about what we have to do next.

Take time in your day to stop the busy-ness in your mind, and either sit quietly     (even if it's only for ten minutes), meditate if you have a practice, or simply life gaze. No one is too busy to take a few minutes to watch a bird fly across the sky, or feel a breeze softly move your hair across your face, or hear the lovely sound of a child laughing, or see the twinkle in an elderly person's eyes to remind you that the spirit is ageless.

Do yourself a favor: Take *"present moment breaks"* from the demands of everyday life. Balance your day with the time you spend performing work, chores or errands, and present moment intervals to stop the monotony of busy-ness. We can spend an entire day caught in the current of "doing" and in our doing, we're not a 100% present.

It's like we're on autopilot, which is how we function most of the time, but we miss so much when we're functioning this way, as opposed to having focused concentration. There are so many things we do where we are performing on autopilot; like riding a bike or driving a car, but even when we're doing those types of things where we don't need to concentrate on how to pedal a bike, or maneuver a car, we can at least take in what we see around us while we're doing it.

When we're present our senses are heightened, and we can enjoy so much more of what we're seeing, hearing, tasting, smelling, and feeling.

Life is like a "Movable Feast"—there is so much to take in. If you don't stop yourself in it and be aware, it will pass you by. As Ernest Hemingway wrote in his memoir of that name, "We would be together and have our books and at night be warm in bed together with the windows open and the stars bright." Ah, that delightful feeling of being in life, and taking in how magical it is! Remember, all moments are magical when we see them as such.

*Note to self:*

*Be present*
*Enjoy the moments*
*Savor them*
*Appreciate being alive in them*
*Feel the magic*

# CHAPTER 5

# The Future

*True happiness is... to enjoy the present, without anxious*
*dependence upon the future.*
*—Lucius Annaeus Seneca*

Here's what we know for certain about the future: It isn't here yet. We can imagine it, predict it, and even dread it, and although we can help plan for it—and hope that it will turn out exactly as we would like it to—the future comes, as it will. We want to welcome it by being ready, and that means being fully present when it arrives, and accepting what it brings with it.

The past may cause us unhappiness because we lament what we wish had been different, but it is the future that causes us the most unrest or anxiety because we can only speculate, anticipate or fret about what *could* or *might* happen. We can spend—and waste—endless moments worrying about an outcome that most often is completely out of our control.

That doesn't mean we can't prepare for a positive result by putting our best efforts into something in present time consciously and mindfully, but if we do things just for the end result or payoff, then we aren't really living fully in the present. Instead, we always have one foot out of the moment, which is more like hopping along in life rather than walking with your feet firmly planted in each moment like you own them, carrying yourself in each one with confidence and grace.

There are people who live half in the present, and half in the future, and what ends up happening is that they're split in their commitment to the present. It's like they're here, sort of, or kind of, or not really, and for people who are very present in the moment, they can sense it, and it can come off as indifferent, inattentive, distracted, and even disrespectful. You know those people who are talking to you, and instead of staying fixed on your eyes, they're looking over your shoulder, more interested in who *might* come into the room and *could* be more interesting or captivating than you. Talk about insulting!

And that's exactly how it comes across when you're not present, especially around other people. Not being present can actually be rude. So next time you want to avoid or disappear out of a moment, keep in mind people may be watching.

By practicing Mindfulness, which is being in the present moment with total awareness, you become more cognizant of when you are slipping out of the moment, catch it, and bring yourself right back to it.

An example might be when you're about to leave the house and you're in a hurry. You say goodbye to your partner or child without looking them in the eye and connecting with them. Even if you're halfway out the door, catch yourself having not been present in that moment, then turn around if you can, and say goodbye mindfully. Or, at the very least, tell yourself you'll apologize to them for having not been present the first opportunity you get.

People really appreciate it when we acknowledge our lack of Mindfulness. Often, we are able to make up for it at a later time, which can make a big difference to someone we were not mindful with in a moment we could have been. It's better to catch it as close to the time when it happens, but anytime we acknowledge our actions, either to ourselves or someone else, it will certainly help strengthen our Mindfulness more than before.

I call this **Mindfulness Repair.** *It can help salvage a moment of thoughtless behavior, or an action you took with another person that could have hurt or offended them. It's a helpful remedy to do in the present to strengthen your Mindfulness so that you don't carry inconsiderate or unmindful behavior into the future.*

Here are some examples where we can fall into the trap of not being mindful, and implement Mindfulness Repair quickly if we can:

1.  Being rude to a server like a waiter or a salesperson.

2.  Talking down to someone you think is beneath you or inferior.

3.  Ignoring someone in your presence like at a meeting, gathering or a party.

4.  Not introducing someone to another person, unless you've forgotten their name, which you can honestly admit if you feel comfortable.

5.  Not including someone in a conversation.

6.  Talking over someone and not being a good listener.

7.  Being impatient and snapping at someone quickly.

8.  Butting in line or rushing to get in front of someone.

9.  Cutting someone off in traffic.

10. Not showing someone appreciation, or thanking them for something they've done for you.

11.   Not returning someone's calls or emails in a timely manner, and explaining why you couldn't.

12.   Being late or always cancelling last minute.


These are just some examples of where we can act thoughtlessly, but clearly there are many more that can fall into the category of lacking Mindfulness. Sometimes we aren't even aware of when we are acting inconsiderately or being insensitive to someone else, and the key with strengthening our Mindfulness skills is to catch ourselves when we forget to do it; and making an effort to get better at it.

Remember, even if you can't salvage or repair something you said or did right away when it happened, it's still important to be able to reflect on how else you could have behaved, or said something differently, be it nicer or with more attentiveness. Look, we're going to have those moments that fall through the cracks, and hopefully we'll catch them quickly to bring ourselves back to a moment, and get right back on the Mindfulness track. It's as important to catch yourself slipping out of a moment as it is keeping yourself in it. Making an effort to stay present, and not wanting to jump into future moments deserves acknowledgement. If you're someone who's really committed to staying more present, and being more mindful, you'll realize how important it is to be kind to yourself in the process.

By practicing Mindfulness consistently, you will also get proficient at sensing when you want to, or are choosing to abandon a moment (and even the person you're with). There will be those times when you are very aware of how much you want to be out of the moment you are in, and hurry to the next one, but out of kindness, you will be present and do it mindfully, which will come across in your energy, and behavior.

Of course, there will be times that you will find yourself wanting to get out of a moment you are in that is dissatisfying, boring, or even feel like it's wasting your time, which you have every right to decide. But if you're hurrying to get out of a moment by not being mindful of how you're behaving or coming across, you can actually draw the moment out longer, making it more unpleasant than it needs to be, and that's when a moment can feel like it's lasting forever.

When we're mindful, we are bringing something positive to the moment we are in, and even if it's an unpleasant one. Our decision to add to the moment, or even take it higher, can actually transform a moment into something better than something uncomfortable or unlikable.

I'm not saying that each and every moment has to be something more than it is. As a matter of fact, some moments are just downright boring, tedious, horrible, or even repulsive to us, and we can't wait to get to the next one, in hopes that it will be better.

But when we choose to go out of present moment awareness, and not be mindful of our discomfort, or objecting to the moment we are in, we are going to be at the effect of it, and basically surrender to the unpleasantness rather than trying to work with it. *We always have a choice about how we want to be in a moment*, and if we're going to constantly want to be out of the present because we anticipate that another (future) moment is going to be better, or we just have a hard time being present because the present moment doesn't ever seem like it's enough, or fully satisfying, then we're going to live our life as a ***future chaser*** rather than a ***present experiencer***. And if you're someone who likes to spend more of your time mulling, rethinking or begrudging the past, then you're living your life as a ***past dweller***. Do you fall into any of those categories? Take a look at the following and see:

## Future Chaser:

1. You anticipate the future often.

2. You're usually impatient with the present.

3. You feel anxious about the future.

4. You get bored quickly with the present.

5. You think the future will be better than the present.

## Past Dweller:

1. You live mostly in the past.

2. You think the past was better than the present.

3.  You long for what "once was."

4.  You wish you could change your past.

5.  You hold onto resentment of what happened in the past.

6.  You keep trying to change the past in your mind.

## Present Experiencer:

1.  You are the happiest in the present.

2.  You enjoy showing up for the moments of your life.

3.  You allow yourself to fully experience whatever you're doing in the present.

4.  You don't think about the past that much except with fond memories.

5.  You let whatever unpleasant experiences you had in the past, go.

6.  You value the present.

So, ask yourself: which moment or period of time do you like to hang out most in—past, present or future?

Whether we're aware of it or not, our mind can jump to the past or present often, and by being mindful of its tendency to wander, we can catch it, and bring it back to the present moment. But what I want to focus on mostly in this chapter is our tendency to put our attention onto the future, and, as I said, to anticipate what "might" or "could" happen.

Remember: what *is* certain is that someone who is living fully in the present is going to get a lot more out of life than someone who's not.

# *Benefits to Living in the Present Moment:*

You're more awake.

You're more aware.

You're more conscious.

You're more focused.

You're more creative.

Your senses are heightened.

You can taste your food better.

You can hear better.

You're more perceptive.

You value your time.

You value other people's time.

You feel more abundant.

You feel more satisfied.

You feel less restless.

You can see more clearly.

You can feel more deeply.

You're kinder.

You're more compassionate.

You're more sensitive.

You're less selfish.

You're more discerning.

You're more cognizant.

You're more accepting.

You're less judgmental.

You're less anxious.

You're more peaceful.

You feel more connected.

You're happier.

# *Detriments of Living in the Future:*

You're more rushed.

You're unfocused.

You're dissatisfied.

You're frustrated.

You're anxious.

You're discontent.

You're restless.

You're agitated.

You're moody.

You're impatient.

You're rude.

You're more fearful.

You're less reachable.

You're emotionally unavailable.

You can feel empty inside.

You can feel more worried.

You can feel distrustful.

You can feel misunderstood.

You don't get your needs met.

You can't meet other people's needs.

It's harder to have a successful relationship.

It's harder to keep a job.

You can't connect to your purpose.

You feel disconnected.

You feel isolated.

You feel lonely.

You're less happy.

We often don't always realize how "out of the moment" we really are. Even when we are doing a pleasurable activity like watching a movie, driving a car, or having sex, our mind can be anywhere but in the moment of now. That doesn't mean we're not in the present physically, because clearly we have to be if we're doing any of those things, but if our mind is elsewhere, it's our body that's showing up more than our mind.

Think about that for a moment (yes, a moment is needed here to make sense of this)—doing something like having sex with your mind elsewhere is like going through the motions with your heart and soul in another room! Among the many problems with that is the person who's on the receiving end will most likely sense it, and feel hurt by it. What you end up experiencing is mechanical love-making, which definitely cannot compare to being fully intimate with someone—mind, body and spirit—in the present.

So, check in with yourself to find out if you're being a **past dweller**, **present experiencer,** or a **future catcher**. If you find yourself trying to slip out the back door of a moment, and jump into another one, either the past or the future, at least be honest about it. If you don't feel like you can really show up for a moment, then at least fess up to it.

Admit it to yourself by saying, *"I'm not really here right now."* Then continue by asking yourself, *"Where am I?"*

It could be that you don't want to be where you find yourself. That could mean you genuinely don't want to be doing what you're experiencing, or maybe even be with the person you're having the experience with. And that's okay. You're just being honest and authentic with yourself.

But what's really important to know is that by trying to avoid or run away from a moment, it will only make you feel like that moment keeps repeating itself over and over again, like Groundhog Day. So, it's better to live your moments honestly, authentically, and face whatever is going on in the "here and now". And if it's not making you happy, then maybe it's time to take a closer look at what's really bothering you by being even more present to figure it out, and do what you need to change it.

There's a famous saying by Confucius: "No matter where you go, there you are." There are no truer words to describe that if you don't take care of your business in the present, your business will follow you wherever you go, and that means taking the problems of your present right into your future. But your future will always work a lot better if you don't drag unresolved baggage and issues from your past or your present into it.

The future is something to look forward to, not a place to escape to, and even if you like to dream or fantasize about what lies ahead for you, do it mindfully. Be conscious about what you want to create for yourself in the days ahead, and be clear about what your intentions are. There's nothing wrong with thinking about a beautiful future ahead. You deserve the absolute best future possible.

But make your present moments the best they can be, and you will reap the benefits of what you got out of them and learned, which you can carry into all the moments that follow them. Don't spend too much of your time thinking about the future. As Albert Einstein famously said, "I never think of the future—it comes soon enough." That's good advice.

# Meditation for the Future

1. Sit somewhere quiet.

2. Close your eyes.

3. Be aware of any sounds, feeling, thoughts, or sensations in your body. Simply observe them.

4. Put your focus and awareness onto your breath.

5. Take a few deep breaths in and out.

6. Say silently, "I am aware of the future."

7. Say silently, "I don't need to be there."

8. Say silently, "I trust what the future holds for me."

9. Say silently, "I am in the present."

10. Say silently, "My focus and awareness are in this moment."

11. Say silently, "This moment is enough."

12. Bring your focus and awareness back to your body.

13. Slowly open your eyes.

14. *Take as much time as you need to transition out of your meditation.*

### *Note to self:*

**I am here**
**I am present**
**There is no other time than now**

# CHAPTER 6

# **Today**

*Change your life today.*
*Don't gamble on the future, act now, without delay.*
*—Simone de Beauvoir*

When we hear sayings like, "Today is the first day of the rest of your life," we may think, brimming with positivity, "That is so true!" But in a matter of just a few minutes we may find ourselves back to our usual "out of the moment" behavior: today is just another day and the rest of our life is a long ways away. But today really can be the first day of your life because when you live in the present, everything begins in the "now" and the now is all there is. So why not make it a great new beginning.

What's exciting about waking up to today is that we can make great changes in our lives, and today can be the day to do that. That means you can literally get out of bed and decide that you're going to change your life by exercising more, eating better, get a new job, end your relationship, move, get a dog, cut your hair, travel, recycle, or whatever else you really want to do. And then, bam! All of a sudden doubt or insecurity seeps in, and you begin to step away from the idea of today being the first day of your new life, and accept that today is just today, and why should it be different than any other day before it. But it can if you believe it.

The reason why today doesn't get met with a belief in what is possible more often, is that we don't meet it with the awareness of believing in ourselves. We're not fully awake to that idea.

Remember, Mindfulness is being fully present in the moment with total awareness, but if you're not aware of what you're thinking or believing about yourself in the moment of *now*, then you're living in this very moment with old ideas, opinions or beliefs about yourself, and they're going to be very real for you in the present, whether you know it or not.

When you're living your life as a *past dweller* it's easy to carry into today the "same ol' same ol'" beliefs about ourselves. Some of those beliefs may be, "Nothing ever works out for me," or "Why should I bother?" or "I'm never going to lose weight" or "I'll never meet my soul-mate" or "I'll never get pregnant" or "I'll never find that great job" or "I'll never be successful" and on and on and on.

You may think you're out of the past, but that doesn't mean your beliefs are.

So much of what we carry over into the present is what we've been telling ourselves—that inner voice—for so long. Unless we change that inner "I'm not good enough" or "I don't deserve better" talk, today will be just another day, and our past dweller babble, or what I like to call the "yeah buts" will run the show and dictate exactly how today is going to go.

When you make the decision to make today different than any other day before it, you have to also decide to not let your past negative beliefs about yourself get in the way of the changes that can happen today in the now.

Now is now, and today is today. There has never been another "now" and there has never been another "today" nor will there ever be again. This is it!  Right now literally means, right this very moment, so seize it! Grab it like you really want it, and deserve it. And don't let it slip through your fingers.

You may tell yourself you're not good enough, or not this enough/that enough, or remind yourself that you're fat, or ugly, or weak, or unlovable, or a loser, or whatever berating, demeaning, and downright awful thing you want to tell yourself over and over again, but if you really want today to matter, and be different than any other day you've ever lived before it, begin now, and really do it because you can. There's that doubt again! You probably just told yourself something that you've told yourself so many times before. But guess what, all that's going to change because you're going to change it today.

So how do you do that? You begin by catching yourself slipping out of the moment, which I referred to earlier, and bringing yourself right back to it. That means the second your mind starts to wander to *past dweller* or *future chaser* negative talk, you catch it immediately and do the following:

- Acknowledge your awareness of slipping out of the present moment.

- Be aware of any harsh opinions of yourself.

- Say any of the following affirmations:

  - ✓ "I am present in this moment with kindness, love and acceptance."

  - ✓ "Today is different than any other day before it."

  - ✓ "The past is gone, the future is not here yet, and the present is here to manifest what I want."

  - ✓ "I believe in myself."

  - ✓ "I believe in what I want to manifest."

  - ✓ "Who I was then is not who I am today."

  - ✓ "Who I am today is capable of manifesting positive, healthy things for myself."

✓ "I am ready to manifest a great today."

✓ "Today begins now."


The only way for today to be unlike any other day is for you to take hold of it by the reins, and guide it to where you want it to go. You're the one on top of the "happy trails" horse, and you can't ride that horse if your mind is elsewhere because that horse is going to sense that you're not in control and want to buck you right off it.

Make today the first day of your new life. This is it. This is the one that matters the most because it's the day you're alive in, and tomorrow may never come. What are you waiting for? Don't let today come and go and find yourself thinking tomorrow, "would-a could-a should-a." That would be a total waste of "all moments are golden" energy.

Value your moments—they are what constitute your Today. They offer you the oxygen that keeps your heart pumping, and breathes life into your very existence. Each one of them is ready to serve you as you want them to, but they can't work alone if you're not fully available for them to support you, or grateful for how much they want you to succeed. Live today unlike you've ever lived another day before it.

Are you ready?

# Today Meditation

1.  Sit somewhere quiet.

2.  Close your eyes.

3.  Be aware of any sounds, thoughts, feelings, or sensations in your body. Simply observe them.

4.  Put your focus and awareness onto your breath.

5.  Take a few deep breaths in and out.

6.  Say silently, "I am alive today."

7.  Say silently, "Today is all that matters."

8.  Say silently, "I am grateful for today."

9.  Say silently, "I wish to live today to its fullest."

10. Bring your focus and awareness back to your body.

11. Slowly open your eyes.

12. *Take the time you need to transition out of your meditation.*

*Note to self:*

*Hello today*
*I'm so glad you're here*
*I'm ready for you*

# PART II

# Understanding

*After all, without understanding yourself,*
*What basis have you for right thinking?*
*—Jiddu Krishnamurti*

# CHAPTER 7

# Wholeness

*To be great, be whole;*
*Exclude nothing, exaggerate nothing that is not you.*
*Be whole in everything. Put all you are*
*Into the smallest thing you do.*
*So, in each lake, the moon shines with splendor*
*Because it blooms up above.*
*—Fernando Pessoa*

When we live in the present moment with acceptance, practice Mindfulness, don't dwell in the past, and not chase the future, we can begin to experience a feeling of **wholeness**, which means we are at one with ourselves—

mind, body, and spirit. Wholeness can also be described as "oneness" which is a state of being "unified or whole" with everything, but I believe that unless you connect to the wholeness of your own being first, you cannot connect to the wholeness of "everything."

My goal is to help you reach that state of oneness, which is not feeling separate from anyone or anything, and I plan to drop you off there at the end of this book so you can begin exploring that further yourself. But let's first look at what wholeness really means before we jump ahead of ourselves to something that will come when we are ready to experience it.

Wholeness, for me, is being who I really am, which again, is the ***authentic self***. I know that it's hard to sustain that state of being because, as I've been saying, it requires us to be fully present with ourselves all the time, and that is our greatest challenge.

Many people who meditate say they experience that feeling of total contentment, and being at "one" with themselves when they sit quietly. It can feel as if you are no longer just a person (self) sitting in meditation, but rather selfless, and connected to something that can be described as "everything." That feeling may very well be a glimpse into total oneness, but it seems temporary and ephemeral, only to be experienced during meditation.

The reason for that is we not only have a hard time staying in the present moment, but we also live, for the most part, in a dualistic state, meaning that we exist in a reality of contrasts or opposites: dark and light, good and bad, positive and negative, material and spiritual; and when we try to make meaning of these opposites, and the different pulls we feel daily because of them, this is when we separate ourselves from things, or others, because we see ourselves as different from them.

Are we good, or are we bad? Are we light, or are we dark? Are we spiritual or are we material? We are everything, which means we have all aspects and characteristics that everyone else has, whether we want to admit it or not.

The problem is we can project the darker aspects of ourselves—what psychoanalyst Carl Jung called the "shadow"—onto others. But, as Jung emphasizes, until we own our own darkness, "We won't know the best method for dealing with others' darkness."

And if we understand that we are, as French philosopher Pierre Teilhard de Chardin said, "spiritual beings having a human experience," we can recognize that we have some catching up to do with our higher self, because the body is also full of contrasts—fragile, yet strong; agile, yet clumsy. And even though we may feel invincible, we are mere mortals finding our way to a more spiritual way of being.

So how do you live your life knowing that this wholeness exists in you, and it's hard, not only to access it, but to sustain it? We've established that it's difficult enough to stay in the moment, let alone figure out a way to let our "human experience" make room for our "spiritual being." A moment is not very long. You have to admit it goes by rather quickly, so how in the world is your spirit going to get a chance to make its presence known in such a short period of time?

The answer is: You commit to being present, and your spiritual being will find its way through. It needs you to make room for it to come forward.

If you're so busy having your "human experience" and taking care of all your human needs, and feeding them through pleasure and satisfaction, then you're not allowing your spiritual being to lead the way. And it needs to. It is our "spiritual being" in our "human experience" that must be with us in every single moment of our life. If we think that being present is for any other reason than realizing a more spiritual and conscious way of being, we're kidding ourselves. And expecting the moments of our lives to make our human experience an enjoyable one by supplying us with material things or stuff, we need to seriously ask ourselves: how much more stuff do we need? And will it bring us peace and fulfillment?

Each moment is an opportunity to allow for the spiritual to shine through our "human experience". By doing so, we can then open ourselves up to the possibility of feeling an ever-present wholeness within us.

### *Here is what you can do today for that to happen:*

Be present
Practice Mindfulness
Sit quietly or meditate
Observe your inner dialogue
Catch yourself escaping the present
Be honest when you are not present
Bring yourself back to the present

Take present moment breaks
Life gaze
Make room for your "spiritual being" in your
"human experience"

Although an ever-present wholeness exists in our true nature, we must find our way back to it again and again because we are constantly at the effect of the duality that is all around us, and in us. We're in the moment / we're out of the moment. We're connected to our wholeness / we feel scattered and fragmented. Such is life. But the farther we move away from being present, the harder it is to find our way back home to our most true, authentic self.

By making a commitment to Mindfulness, and staying present as often as you can, you will hold on to that feeling of wholeness, and soon you will find it is with you more often, or should I say, you and "it" will function as one.

# Meditation for Wholeness

1. Sit somewhere quiet.

2. Gently close your eyes.

3. Be aware of any sounds, thoughts, feelings or sensations in your body. Simply observe them.

4. Put your focus and awareness onto your breath.

5. Take a few deep breaths in and out.

6. Say silently, "I am whole."

7. Say silently, "I am complete."

8. Say silently, "I am at one with myself."

9. Bring your focus and awareness back to your body.

10. Slowly open your eyes.

11. *Take the time you need to transition out of your meditation.*

*Note to self:*

*I am present*
*I am in the now*
*I am a spiritual being*
*I am having a human experience*

# CHAPTER 8

# Coexistence

*The only alternative to coexistence is codestruction.*
—*Jawaharlal Nehru*

*It's coexistence or no existence.*
—*Bertrand Russell*

I f our true nature is wholeness, which is being "unbroken or damaged", and we can experience it in the oneness of all that exists, how can we connect to that in others, and function in our oneness together? Ah, such is the biggest challenge of this lifetime! That's why practicing Mindfulness and learning how to be present so that our "spiritual being" can shine through our "human experience" is so vitally important.

Which, of course (as we've discussed), means that what you do with your today, and what I do with my today, will affect all of the todays of everyone on the planet.

So, if you're living your life committed to being present, and prefer being awake and aware instead of being asleep at the wheel of your life journey, then we stand a greater chance of **coexisting** consciously, instead of letting our "human experience" run the show, and broadsiding each other in our unconsciousness along the way.

At its very essence, to coexist means, "We exist in mutual tolerance despite different ideologies or interests."

Okay, so how do we do that? I mean, if we have a hard time accepting ourselves with love and tolerance, how can we accept or tolerate each other's differences? It sure doesn't seem like we're doing such a great job of it lately, and it's not at all surprising. The reason is that if we're having a hard time staying present and awake, and are thus unaware of our own intolerance of ourselves, then we live our life unconscious of the fact that we are acting out on others.

Remember what I said in Chapter 4 (The Present): "When we're unaware of ourselves in a moment, it's easy to respond or react to what's going on unconsciously." And that's exactly how we're behaving towards one another most of the time; unconsciously.

We're not always bringing our best selves forward, let alone offering up our "spiritual being." We are so busy slipping in and out of the present moment like yo-yos, and functioning out of fear that someone will get ahead of us, or do better than us, or have more than us, or attack us first, that we're functioning not only as *future catchers*, but more like **future mongers**, which I think is pretty self-explanatory.

Where the past can be helpful for this is remembering what we learned from it, but unfortunately that's not what we usually use the past for. Instead we'd rather resent or blame others for our past, and let it fuel us in the present so we can retaliate at whoever we think wronged us, and show them who's boss, in case they think they can outdo us in the future.

And that is why the only way to stop all the madness (and I think we can all agree that today's climate is, indeed, madness), is to find the wholeness within ourselves. And there is no other way to do that than by being present, and checking in to see how awake and aware we are, and if our "spiritual being" is anywhere in sight.

We can't possibly stand a chance of coexisting if we continue to be split between ourselves. If we don't commit to finding our way back to our inherent wholeness, we will continue to live our lives "broken" and "damaged" by our ignorance.

Each one of us has the potential to become whole again, but we must be willing to do the work, which means being present—right here, right now, in this moment, seeing it for what it is, and doing what we need to do to repair the damage we've done by not being present when we created it in the first place.

You can't pollute the planet consciously. You can't rob people of their rights consciously. You can't abuse someone consciously. You can't lie to people consciously. You can't steal from the poor consciously. You can't watch people suffer consciously. You just can't do it. When you're conscious, you do conscious things, and you act consciously, and you behave consciously, and you stand up for consciousness because you know that being a conscious human being is the only way to live. Not living that way is not caring about anyone other than yourself, and that is selfishness personified.

I'm talking about our ability to feel and care for one another; our fundamental humanity. How can we co-exist if we don't value our fellow man? It seems as if we've been living in a giant, colossal snooze bubble, and it is seriously time for us to wake up. Let us begin with a Meditation for Coexisting.

# Meditation for Coexisting

*(You can say all of the affirmations, or just one, and repeat at any other time in your day)*

1.  Sit somewhere quiet.

2.  Close your eyes.

3.  Be aware of any sounds, thoughts, feelings or sensations in your body. Simply observe them.

4.  Put your focus and awareness on your breath.

5.  Take a few deep breaths in and out.

6.  If at any time your mind begins to wander, bring your focus back to your breath.

7.  Say silently, "I accept myself."

8.  Say silently, "I love myself."

9.  Say silently, "I am tolerant."

10. Say silently, "I accept others."

11. Say silently, "I have the capacity to love others."

12. Say silently, "I am tolerant of others."

13. Say silently, "I can coexist with others."

14. Say silently, "I wish for love and peace on the planet."

15. Say silently, "I have compassion for all living beings and creatures."

16. Say silently, "I wish to awaken to each moment I am in."

17. Say silently, "I wish to shine my light outward to the rest of the world."

18. Say silently, "I wish to live my life with clear intentions, and be in service for creating a better world for all."

19. Say silently, "I am committed to being present in this moment and all of the moments of my life."

20. Bring your focus and awareness back to your body.

21. Slowly open your eyes.

22. *When you are ready, transition out of your meditation.*

Here is a lovely poem by Rumi to remind us of our "oneness":

*One Song*

*All religions*
*All this singing*
*Is one song.*

*The differences are just*
*Illusion and vanity.*

*The sun's light looks a little different*
*On this wall than it does on that wall,*
*And a lot different on this other one,*
*But it's still one light.*

*We have borrowed these clothes,*
*These time and place personalities*
*From a light, and when we praise,*
*We're pouring them back in.*

*Note to self:*

*I am present*
*I am light*
*I am love*
*I am tolerant*
*I am accepting*
*I am whole*
*I coexist*

# CHAPTER 9

# Consciousness

*The key to growth is the introduction of higher*
*dimensions of consciousness into our awareness.*
—*Lao Tzu*

I said in the previous chapter, you can't do hurtful or harmful things to people "consciously". However, people can—and have—done bad things to good people, as evident by the atrocities done to six million innocent Jews in the Holocaust.

But I believe there are different levels of conscious awareness. If someone is not connected to their wholeness, they can function from a place in them that is "broken" or "damaged" and might be completely unaware that they are.

When Jesus says, "Father, forgive them for they know not what they do," it says so much about the "transgressions" man is capable of, and the more he is unaware of his wrong-doings or sins, the greater those offenses can be.

You can only function from a level of awareness you are on, and if that level is low, you will operate from a lower, or baser level of consciousness, and if you act from a higher level, it is the consciousness of your higher self that is present.

Higher consciousness is a state of "elevated awareness." But as I said earlier, we function more often than not from an unaware place because we are not in a state of Mindfulness; that is, being present with total awareness.

You may be conscious that you are polluting the planet by not recycling, and might not really care, but that means you are either choosing not to care, or don't care enough to raise your awareness about it. But if you do, you will automatically heighten your awareness even more, which will then raise your consciousness, and that most likely will make you rethink the importance of recycling, and your role in helping to take care of the planet.

So, you can see how raising the bar on consciousness works, which can be a pretty rewarding way to live your life. If you're someone who likes to learn, grow, and evolve, I highly recommend trying the *raise your consciousness challenge*, which is aspiring to be a more evolved and compassionate human being on the planet, and the great reward for that is you will be that much closer to enlightenment, which according to Buddhism is reaching Nirvana, "a place of perfect peace and happiness, like heaven." But we've got a lot of consciousness raising work to do before we can realize that ultimate state of bliss, and a good place to start is rolling up your sleeves and practice Mindfulness daily, and do it with consistency.

The road to enlightenment might be a very long one, and as we know, it took Buddha approximately six to ten years just to learn the best way to meditate before he sat under the Bodhi tree for seven straight days without moving, and then became enlightened. But we don't know what stages of consciousness he went through to reach that ultimate state, meaning the different levels of awareness he experienced, which could have been hundreds or thousands of stages, and what he taught us was, "consciousness is always continuing, like a stream of water."

The encouraging news is that this is a journey each one of us can take, one moment at a time. And who knows what states of awareness or consciousness we can realize along the way too? But the best way to raise our awareness is to be willing to do things that help heighten or develop it. And even if that means just doing one thing that makes us more mindful, we are continuing to stay on the path of enlightenment, like the Buddha did, one step at a time.

Here are a few suggestions for the "Raise Your Consciousness Challenge", which is a great way to stay on the path of awareness and compassion:

1. Be informed about what's going on. That means don't bury your head in the sand, but be aware of what's happening in as many areas as you can, such

as politics, the environment, underserved, etc. and see where you can get involved.

2. Care for the elderly. If you have parents or a relative who is alive, check in with them daily, or try and see them as often as you can if they live nearby. If you don't have elderly parents or a relative to care for, maybe you have an elderly neighbor you could visit or bring food to.

3. Volunteer. Find time to lend your help to a charity, mental health facility, hospital, the VA, the mission, or any place you can contribute your assistance or aid.

4. Donate. Clean out your closets and let go of clothes, shoes or jewelry you no longer use or need, or kitchen supplies. It feels good to let go of things we aren't using, especially knowing someone might need it more than you do. Giving to a blood bank is another way to donate, and is much needed.

5. Adopt a rescue animal. There is such an overpopulation of animals, and thousands of them are euthanized daily. Taking one into your home can be such a heart fulfilling experience for you and your family, if you have one.

6. Be there for someone who needs your help. Offer to care for or tend to a friend who just had surgery, is going through a divorce, quit their job, or is in some

type of transition or crisis. Not everyone's comfortable asking for help so it's good to initiate and find out if they do.

7. Consider fostering a child. There are nearly 500,000 children in Foster Care in the United States, and if you don't have children, or your children are grown, caring for a child could be something that could be deeply satisfying for you, and give a child the care and love they desperately need.

8. And finally, think of one thing you can do daily that makes you more conscious or heightens your awareness. That could be anything from vowing not to gossip, or making a concerted effort to smile at one stranger a day. When you are in the mind-set of raising your consciousness, acts of kindness and compassion will come easier for you, and will find yourself thinking of ways you can express it.

There really are so many things we can do that can contribute to raising our consciousness, and it takes very little effort to commit to at least one thing a day. Taking the *Raising Your Consciousness Challenge* really means that you are committed to things like Mindfulness, and waking up each day not just thinking of yourself, but thinking of how you can help others. If each of us did that, imagine how much more conscious the world would be.

Committing to self-care is another way to help raise our consciousness. Finding time to stop the "doing" as I mentioned, and connect more to our "spiritual being" will always bring us back to the inner dwelling of our wholeness, which, in essence, is the authentic self. Taking time to connect to and acknowledge our true nature is saying to ourselves, "I recognize that which is worthy, divine and holy in myself."

If we don't recognize and respect what is most real, pure and good in ourselves, how can we recognize and respect it in another? The word "Namaste" means: "My soul recognizes your soul. I honor the light, love, beauty, truth and kindness within you because it is also in me. In sharing these things there is no distance and no difference between us, we are the same, we are one." I suggest giving yourself a nice, warm "Namaste" first thing every morning.

### *Sitting in meditation is a great way to heighten our awareness, and raise our consciousness.*

As I said, many people feel that meditation is where they connect with the wholeness that is within them the best, but it doesn't have to be the only place. We can experience that feeling when we take a walk and connect to nature, or when we sit quietly having a cup of tea, or taking a relaxing bath. When we are fully present, and are surrendered to a moment with total awareness, we can experience a sense of non-separation, and that is when we can feel whole and complete.

But again, in order for that to happen we need to stop the "doing" and make more time for "being" present in a moment. It is in our being-ness that we can let our awareness soar.

# Meditation to Connect to Consciousness

1.  Sit somewhere quiet.

2.  Close your eyes.

3.  Be aware of any sounds, thoughts, feelings or sensations in your body. Simply observe them.

4.  Put your focus and awareness on your breath.

5.  Take a few deep breaths in and out.

6.  Say silently, "I am alive."

7.  Say silently, "I am breathing."

8.  Say silently, "I am connected to all that exists."

9.  Say quietly one, or any of the following:

    - ⚘ "I am the universe."

    - ⚘ "I am timeless."

    - ⚘ "I am eternal."

    - ⚘ "I am light."

    - ⚘ "I am love.

    - ⚘ "I am whole."

    - ⚘ "I am one."

10. When you are ready bring your awareness back to your body.

11. Slowly open your eyes.

12. *Take your time to transition out of your meditation.*

*As in the stillness of the mind*
*I saw myself as I am—unbound.*
*—Sri Nisargadatta Maharaj*

Ultimately, consciousness is being aware of everything: you, others, nature, animals, the sky, birds, sounds, thoughts, feelings, sensations, and all that exits. When we stay in the moment with awareness, we are able to observe ourselves in how we are being, responding, or reacting to everything. Are we being kind, are we being thoughtful, are we being compassionate, are we loving ourselves, first and foremost, and then others?

Remember: We have a choice at every given moment to decide who we are, and how we want to be in our consciousness. As elusive or mysterious as consciousness can be—for it has intrigued, as well as baffled philosophers and some of the greatest thinkers and sages, perhaps because it is "always continuing, like a stream of water" and basically has no end—we still can decide how we want to live it, depending on what it personally means to us. Nobody can tell us what consciousness means to us, because it's different for each and every person. It could mean something spiritual, or scientific, or abstract, or absolutely nothing to you. *That's right, consciousness can mean "nothing."* But where my mind goes with that is that even in "nothing" there is "something" and in something, there is *everything*.

You can make of consciousness what you choose to, if it's something you wish to know more about. If you come up with an idea about it that you think is insightful or illuminating, share it with others—because we are all on this consciousness raising journey together, and can help each other awaken by our own awakening along the way.

*Note to self:*

*I am awake*
*I am aware*
*I am me*
*I am you*
*I am everything*

# CHAPTER 10

# Self

*There is only one corner of the universe you can be*
*certain of improving, and that's your own self.*
—*Aldous Huxley*

When we speak about consciousness, it can feel like
we're delving into territory that is boundless and
immeasurable. And by thinking of ourselves as connected
to everything, including the never-ending universe, we can
imagine ourselves as part of the cosmos, and that there is
no beginning or end to our existence, which is pretty trippy.
But it can also make us feel tiny and insignificant, like a
speck in the infinite, which is invisible.

I love Carl Sagan's quote, "We are all made of star-stuff," which for me says how huge we really are. Then when he says, "We are a way for the cosmos to know itself," it makes me feel that my role in the vast universe is important, and that through understanding who I am better, I can then understand the mystery of existence, and let existence know about my findings. I think the idea of having an intimate relationship with the cosmos is pretty cool. And letting it in on my ideas, or theories of what I think the universe is, excites me. We may not think the universe is listening, but who cares.

If we believe we have something valuable or interesting to say about why we're here, or how we got here, or what we're doing here, and who played a role in creating this cosmic playground, why not share it with whoever wants to listen? And if the universe listens, great, and if not, that's okay too.

So, I feel like it's up to me to decide how well I want to get to know myself, and based on what I find out, it will determine how much better I understand the meaning of my life and my purpose here. All of us can benefit from this, and I can only hope you find this as exciting and as sexy as I do. Sexy might seem like an odd word to describe getting to know yourself, but in truth, knowing ourselves in a private and personal way is the highest act of intimacy we can have, and that type of intimacy, in my opinion, is sexy.

And we can choose that type of personal intimacy if we really want to get to know ourselves entirely. We can either take a deep-dive into finding out who we really are, or go through life having a more superficial relationship to ourselves, which in essence means that's about as deep as you can go with anybody else. Boring!

Look, it may seem like a tremendous amount of work to get to know ourselves better, but connecting to our true nature—*our authentic self*—sometimes requires us to go a little deeper within, and take a closer look at what's there. The inner journey I've spoken about is the only way we can learn more about who we really are, and that can mean facing what we're uncomfortable with, and that also means questioning the negative and critical thoughts we're telling ourselves.

And if, in our finding out who we are by scuba-diving to the bottom of the deep blue sea of our psyche we discover some wreckage there, and maybe remnants of a sunken ship, we must also remember that there are treasures to be found too. The deeper you go, the more treasures you may find, and they can be the most beautiful things you've ever seen.

As Socrates said, "The unexamined life is not worth living." If you really want to know who you are and what you're made of, you need to do some serious examining, and in order to do that thoroughly, you have to be present, and willing to go within. You can venture into what I call the "**house of self**" like you're about to go on an adventure of a lifetime, but that doesn't mean you're not going to encounter some dark and scary places too. Some people want the Fast Pass to all of the newest and most advanced rides in the theme park, some want things nice and slow, and then there's others who will never go anywhere near the "haunted house." But when you realize that it's not real, and it's just a place "intended" to frighten you, you can see it for what it is, and take your power back from something that appears dark and spooky, but is nothing more than a form of entertainment and distraction.

I use the haunted house as an analogy for the dark room of ourselves, even though it might seem anything but appealing or entertaining, and we may have it locked like a dusty, moldy attic, but it invites us in so that we can air it out, and take a closer look at what's there instead of fearing it. Yes, it can be filled with unpleasant memories, but as I said in Chapter 3 (The Past), "We can either choose to stay stuck in the darkness, or shine a light on what has happened to us, and what we've experienced that has caused us pain and suffering."

We can exchange those horrible images etched in our memory that are like cobwebs or ghouls in a haunted house for images like a sparkle of light dancing across an ocean, or an eagle soaring high in the sky, and envisioning yourself as that majestic bird. It doesn't matter how you take the ride on this life journey, if you choose to go fast or slow. What's important is that you at least be willing to venture forward to see what you may find, and that may mean going into the more dark or complicated places within yourself. But know that along the way, you can treat yourself to some candy or ice-cream, like you would at an actual theme park, to remind you how sweet life can be, even if it can seem overwhelming.

We are as complex as the universe, and our life here on this planet shows us how complex and perplexing we are by what we are creating, and have already manifested.

There is so much going on in this modern, hectic society, and even though we may be "spiritual beings", we are having this thing called a "human experience," and we've made some big mistakes along the way. We've also done some remarkable and extraordinary things, and what we're capable of is nothing short of mind boggling. But by getting to know ourselves better, we can add even more to this life, this world, this universe, and again, that's exciting, and if you agree, *sexy*.

But it all begins with us, and asking; "Who am I?" That one question alone can bring you that much closer to finding out who you really are. Don't you want to know?

There's nothing to fear other than your fear of finding out that you're human, and have insecurities, doubts and concerns just like everyone else, which fuels your fear, and then makes you afraid to find out more about yourself. But if you can't get past the first chapter of the "book of self", which might give you all your negatives or imperfections first, then you're not going to get to the really good part of what makes you unique and special, and different than anyone else on this great big planet, in this never-ending universe, which you are a part of. The cosmos is going to learn from what you have come to know, whether you believe that or not. It's all there in the book of self—which is about *you*.

You are the great, big novel. You are the bestseller. So, read on, and you too can discover more about yourself that you may have forgotten or chosen to bury.

But be present as you turn the pages. Look at every word, every punctuation, every letter. All of what is written about you, you have allowed for. Your life story cannot be told without your approval. If you want to get "cosmic" about it, who's writing your story anyway? Is it you, or is it being written by someone else, and if so, who could that be?

Take a moment and think about that. Don't rush. Really spend some time thinking about who is writing your story? Who knows you better than you do? Who knows that you are both perfect and imperfect because you are part of the struggle of "duality", which each and every person on this planet is dealing with too, and that you're aspiring to be your higher self in spite of the contradictions of having a "human experience." Isn't that perfection?

Isn't there something perfect about how we are becoming our higher self in a slow and deliberate way, and that we didn't just shoot out of the birth canal thinking we know everything there is to ever know, and absolutely nothing we need to learn? What would we be doing here, if not to discover who we are, and what this lifetime means to us?

Maybe we have all the answers in our collective DNA that makes up the higher intelligence of human existence, or maybe it's already encoded in our individual souls. But like someone who has an expensive trust fund, and doesn't have access to it until they're old enough or mature enough to know what to do with it, so may be the hidden or esoteric wisdom that trickles out when we're present or aware enough to access it, and ultimately understand it.

Wisdom shouldn't be given to those who are unconscious because they're not wise enough to interpret it. But, as we know, ancient knowledge and sacred texts have been misinterpreted and rewritten throughout history by the wrong people, and misused to serve the needs of those who wanted to control others to believe what they wanted them to, and some of them did it with the darkest of evil intentions. Hitler inverted the Swastika (Sanskrit svastika), which is a "sacred symbol of spiritual principles in Buddhism, Hinduism, and Janism" and means "good fortune" or "well-being". But because of its misuse, it will forever be in our memories symbolizing the personification of evil, and till today is used in the West by white supremacists to represent racism and hate.

Each of us needs to rise to the level of awareness where we can be the proper interpreters of what is best for ourselves, before we can begin to tell others what we think is best for them, or best for this planet we share.

Let your awareness speak for you. Let people see you as someone who is awake, sharp, and perceptive of what's really going on, and let that ignite awareness in others. As I said earlier, "What you do with your today, and what I do with my today, will effect all of the todays of everyone on this planet."

We are all connected. And this whole cosmic, miraculous, mysterious thing called life is always changing and evolving as we are, and maybe, just maybe we'll get to experience some of the deep inner peace that Buddha did by becoming more awake and aware.

He asked, "Who am I?" and took himself on the path of enlightenment to find out, and it wasn't an easy one. It was an arduous, and probably at times, grueling path of self-discovery; one moment at a time, and you're either committed to the path of awakening or not.

And if you are, begin now. Know the "self" that you are. The you that was who you were when you incarnated into this world, and decided to be here. What was that decision? Can you remember? Was it to be your most real, *authentic* self, or to live your life as someone that you're not? Did you come here to learn? Did you come here to be compassionate? Did you come here to serve?

You are a part of the great "cosmic creation" which is always in process, as are you. So, be kind, be compassionate, and be present in your discovery of "self."

# Meditation for Connecting to Self

1. Sit somewhere quiet.

2. Close your eyes.

3. Be aware of any sounds, feelings, thoughts or sensations in your body, and simply observe them.

4. Focus on your breath.

5. Take a few deep breaths in and out.

6. If your mind begins to wander, bring your focus and awareness back to your breath.

7. Say silently, "Who am I?"

8. Say silently, "Let my true self reveal who I am."

9. Say silently, "Let me realize love, acceptance, non-judgment."

10. When you're ready, bring your focus and awareness back to your body.

11. Slowly open your eyes.

12. *Take the time you need to transition out of your meditation.*

## *Note to self:*

*I am myself*
*I do as I know*
*I know what is true*
*I live as my authentic self*

## CHAPTER 11

# Perception

*If the doors of perception were cleansed every thing*
*would appear to man as it is, infinite.*
*—William Blake*

*In a crooked mind even the right thing gets crooked.*
*—Arsenie Boca*

Our perceptions are based on our beliefs, and those beliefs influence how we see the world, which dictates our sense of reality.

If we're open minded, we'll see the world through a much clearer and wider lens, and be more accepting, tolerant and compassionate. But if we're closed off or small minded, we're not going to be as tolerant, and can make snap judgments before we even give something or someone a chance.

*There's a much more expansive*
*and transcendent way in which we can see things that*
*goes beyond the limitations of beliefs, and that's by*
*being in a state of Mindfulness.*

When we choose to be present and fully aware, we are cognizant of what it is we're seeing and taking in, but we're also aware of *how* we are seeing it and *why*. By being aware of how we are interpreting, or basically sizing up a person or situation, we are doing it with a willingness to keep our mind open to discover and learn more, rather than being unwilling to consider someone else's point of view, or their *perception* of reality. We live in a world where, unfortunately, many people are unwilling to accept each other's viewpoints or beliefs, and the way in which it's addressed is to use anger, hatred and even violence to express their inability to be tolerant of one another's differences.

Everyone has a right to see or perceive as they do, but don't have a right to hurt, harm, or kill because of it.

When our "human experience" is devoid of spiritual meaning, we will do anything to defend our perceptions, which are fueled by more animalistic needs, and that means we are capable of doing heinous things to one another because we are ruled only by greed and fear, and the drive to succeed and survive.

When man lives only caring about, and defending what is best for him, and is unable to tolerate or embrace what another person's needs are (which could be true survival necessities like a roof over one's head, or food to eat), then perhaps life becomes a game of "survival of the fittest", Darwin's evolutionary theory.

Yes, some people are stronger and more fit and able to survive, but if we no longer care about our fellow man, and live each day allowing for, and even participating in the harm or extinction of others less able than us, then we live and exist heartlessly. What a chilling way to go through life.

Have we lost our way from our conscious homeland to such a degree that we perceive one another as a threat to our self-serving need to get ahead, so that we can be superior to someone else?

I know that the dualistic nature of existence is constant, and we've had these issues and problems since the beginning of time. Man's extinction tendencies have been alive in him since he walked this earth. But have we not come a long way from clubbing one another to death over a carcass, and communicating by scratching our armpits and grunting? Sometimes it seems as if we haven't made any true headway in our evolution. Even though we've modernized ourselves materialistically, and created advanced technology like computers that a Neanderthal would have stomped on, at least some of the human population has made great strides in working on themselves psycho-spiritually, and feel that reaching a state of "oneness" is the only way we're going to be able to survive.

But "oneness" can easily be perceived as me-ness, and man will continue to strive to be "at one with" all that is good for him alone. He may have no use or need for the oneness that includes all living beings, and in some people's reality this planet is a place to live, not a place to respect or protect, and the other inhabitants are on their own. And if or when they get in the way, or think differently, or look differently, or need different things, or maybe the same things we all do, but can't afford it, or simply don't have the resources, they can either be controlled, ignored, dismissed or disposed of. Again, so chilling to even think about, and yet this is what's happening daily. Just turn on the news and watch it for yourself. Sometimes it renders you speechless, and causes a deep ache in your heart that we have lost our way so far, that you wonder if we're going to be taken down in a nuclear blast caused by someone in power who has access to real weapons of mass destruction, and is ill equipped or unfit to be anywhere near them.

When life starts to mimic a movie like Stanley Kubrick's "Dr. Strangelove," (if you haven't seen it, I suggest you do to see how accurate art can imitate life) which is about what if the wrong person pushed the wrong button (a fear we have of North Korea leader Kim Jong-un), you know you better start cleaning your perception glasses good and fast, and see things for what they really are, not just what you want to see. Yes, the wrong person can push the wrong button, and go completely insane like crazy General Jack Ripper does in the movie, and they can push it at any time. If we can't perceive who or what is insane, then we are colluding to support a world gone mad.

Time to take off those rose-colored glasses.

But this takes us right back to each of us, and how important it is to know the **house of self** that you live in, and what your perceptions are up to.

If you're not checking in daily with how present, aware and awake you are, then it is far too easy to fall asleep at the wheel, and either you or someone else who's also in an unconscious slumber, will continue to be disruptive and wreak havoc. Those that remain will have to keep pushing this beaten down planet along in hopes that the "awakened" will outnumber the "sleepers", and we can turn this ship around.

Please be a part of the turning, and keep waking up more each day. Stay mindful, be present, clean up your house of self, and make sure your perceptions are spot on and squeaky clean.

See what you are really seeing, and don't use your perception to just see what you want to, or need to, or have to. See what is possible, and see how you can help serve in making this world a much better place. Do it one moment at a time, and each of the moments of your life will add up to a lifetime having been lived with honesty, integrity, courage and, above all, authenticity. And when it is time for you to leave this earth plane, you will know that you were one of the true *consciousness weavers*, and you had a hand in moving this cosmic starship along. We'll get to the land of oneness, and when we do, we'll be ready to live there as we were meant to all along, but not until we raise our consciousness collectively. Remember that "what you do with your today, and what I do with my today, will affect all of the todays of everyone on the planet."

# *Meditation for Perception*

1.  Sit somewhere quiet.

2.  Close your eyes.

3.  Be aware of any sounds, thoughts, feelings or sensations in your body, and simply observe them.

4.  Put your focus and awareness onto your breath.

5.  Take a few deep breaths in and out.

6.  Say silently, "I see."

7.  Say silently, "I see truth."

8.  Say silently, "I see all that is real."

9.  Say silently, "I am aware of my judgments."

10. Say silently, "Let me be tolerant."

11. Say silently, "Let me be compassionate."

12. Say silently, "Let me see others as myself."

13. Bring your focus and awareness back to your body.

14. Slowly open your eyes.

15. *Take your time transitioning out of your meditation.*

## Note to self:

*I see clearly*
*I am tolerant*
*I am compassionate*
*I take responsibility for my perceptions*

# CHAPTER 12

# Thoughts

*As a single footstep will not make a path on the earth, so a single thought will not make a pathway in the mind. To make a deep physical path, we walk again and again. To make a deep mental path, we must think over and over the kind of thoughts we wish to dominate our lives.*
*—Henry David Thoreau*

The most powerful thing about us is our mind, and the thoughts we have in them. As I say in my book, *Says Who?* which includes a method I created for transforming negative and fear-based thoughts, "We are the creator and master of our internal dialogue, which creates our reality." We think approximately up to 70,000 thoughts a day, and some of them are nice, sweet, loving, and productive, but many of them are negative, fearful, critical, mean, and downright useless. But that doesn't mean we don't listen to them, give into them, energize them, and let them have control over us. As a matter of fact, we're inclined to listen to our negative thoughts more than the positive ones because the negative ones are the loudest, and get our attention the most.

We live our lives at the effect of what we are thinking, and if we have thoughts that tell us we're good or capable, that feels nice for the *moment*, and might make us want to pat ourselves on the back, but we are prone to quickly moving past those types of friendly reminders, and seek out the "bad boy" type of thoughts that tell us we're inadequate, or inferior, and probably not going to amount to very much.

Those types of thoughts really know just how to suck us in, and make us doubt ourselves. But when we doubt ourselves we feel less worthy, so we give into the negative thoughts to keep telling us we're not enough, and allow them to set up house in our head, and begin serving them like a king, as we are now our mind's slave.

If you care about creating the reality you want, you know that it's your job to be the author of your life story, as I spoke about in Chapter 10 (Self), and that means you need to be mindful and careful of what you're telling yourself daily.

And if your mind is giving you suggestions or orders, and they're unhealthy or destructive, you need to know that the voices that have taken control in your mind are about to take you down. What can start off as a soft whisper saying;

"Go ahead, have that second piece of cake," or a bossy voice that says, "Take another pill to calm your nerves, you need it," or a jovial voice that says, "Come on, one more drink isn't going to kill you," can end up being the voices that run the show in your head, and before you know it, you've got some negative or even dangerous inner talk going on, and might not realize how at risk you really are for moving towards a downward spiral.

> **Mindfulness keeps you on top of your thinking mind in such a way that you become the gatekeeper of your thoughts.**

It's like having a guard who looks like a monk standing outside the private entrance of your inner sanctum. There's no getting passed him unless your thoughts come bearing gifts like lotus flowers. You are so present that the very first thought that wants to shake things up, or get a party started that can turn into an out of control rave in your head, you immediately kick them out and tell them they're at the wrong address. You have to mean business with your thinking mind, and that means there is no "monkey mind" allowed.

The monkey mind is a Buddhist term meaning "uncontrollable, restless, and confused." That is not what you want happening in your mind. It needs to serve you in the best and most healthy way possible. You are its king, its master, its faithful leader, and never will you lead it down the wrong path because your "spiritual being" knows that the only path to be on is one that supports your wholeness, and suitable for awakening, so therefore your thoughts must be diligent in supporting you to get to what I call "the land of oneness" in your mind.

When you realize there is no king, or boss, or leader, or guru that owns or runs your mind, and that you're it, you need to make sure that you are up for the task.

That means thinking of yourself as someone who's in wisdom school, and like Talmudic scholars who have their faces buried in the ancient texts of Jewish law, it's up to you to form your own solid and wise credos to abide by, and know what kind of smart and productive thoughts you can cultivate to help guide you on a righteous path.

You also have to know that the mind is kind of a troublemaker. Well, actually not "kind of," but a lot. When it's not busy problem solving, inventing cures for something like polio, figuring out how to get a man to the moon, or discovering that the world is round, it looks for bigger and more complex things to solve. It can confuse what feels like a gravitational pull towards negative energy as something important to move closer to and explore, especially if it's not in the present moment, and aware of being pulled towards it. This is why it's important to keep your thoughts positive. If your thoughts are negative, your mind will seek out a similar vibration or frequency to match it because "like attracts like" and that's when you're functioning from a more base or lower-level consciousness instead of your higher self.

The mind likes to be busy. It thrives on activity and distraction, which is why it's incumbent upon us to teach it how to quiet down and be still from time to time, so it can experience what it's like not to be constantly "doing" but can be quiet and peaceful by just "being" and learn how to actually like it. And a more quiet, peaceful mind doesn't seek distraction, or allow for negative thoughts to disrupt its calm state. This, I believe, is the mind's natural stasis, although you wouldn't know it from the trouble it causes, which is why it desperately needs our help to train it.

All of this mental "training" can be very foreign to the mind because it's used to what's familiar and doesn't accept change easily, which is why it's so very important that we help it understand that it does not control us, and that we must tame it, and teach it what it desperately needs to know. As Buddha said, "Rule your mind, or it will rule you." And it most certainly will, if we let it.

What you need to do is stop giving your power away to your mind, which is like enabling it to act badly, or should I say, continue its bad thinking habits that we allow for. We have this tendency to forget that we're the ones that are thinking our thoughts up, both positive and negative, so therefore we have the power to change them, and not hold onto the thoughts that do not support our wellbeing in any way.

If you are giving your power away to your mind, and feel that it's controlling you, and not the other way around, then you're functioning far too much in your "human experience" and not enough in your "spiritual being." When you are aligned with your higher self, you know that your mind is something to master so it doesn't disrupt your inner stillness whenever it feels like it. And as the "creator and master of your internal dialogue, which creates your reality," you get to decide if you want your inner stillness disrupted or not. Yes, it's a choice you have, even if at times it feels like it's not.

The mind can behave like a spoiled child that needs constant attention, and if you don't give it what it wants, or thinks it needs, it will get louder and more disruptive. Imagine it kicking its feet, and pounding its fists on the ground. That's what your mind can act like when it's trying so hard for you to give it what it "thinks" it has to have. That's why meditation is so helpful for quieting the mind. Although it doesn't necessarily stop our thoughts, it helps us pick and choose which ones to let go of. I like to say, "Our thoughts don't hold onto us; we hold onto them."

We send a clear message to our mind in meditation that we're aware of what it's thinking, but we're going to take a break from its mental activity by putting our focus and attention on something else like our breath or a mantra, which tells our mind it can step back and rest with us.

The mind desperately needs that, and we are doing it a huge favor by calming it down.

When you find yourself deeply relaxed in meditation, you know it's working. Some people actually fall asleep, and if you've ever heard someone snore in a meditation class, that's their mind saying, "Thank you for allowing me to take a little break."

The mind definitely needs little thought naps other than when we're sleeping, and even then, it's processing information to help us solve the problems of our day, although we might not remember our dreams when we wake up. It's busy, constantly, and that's why it's important to provide it a much needed, and well-deserved respite at one point in your day. Even if you can't, or choose not to meditate, you want to make sure that you take at least a few minutes to quiet your mind, and send a clear message that it can pause from trying to get something done, or figure something out.

The mind needs to know that we appreciate its best efforts and productivity, but we also need to reward it like an obedient dog with treats, and a perfect reward for the mind is to give it rest and peace sometimes, which it seriously needs.

# Meditation to Quiet Your Thoughts

1. Sit somewhere quiet.

2. Close your eyes.

3. Observe any sounds, thoughts, feelings or sensations you may be experiencing in your body. Simply observe them.

4. Put your focus and awareness onto your breath.

5. Take a few deep breaths in and out.

6. Think of yourself as an observer. There is nothing you need to do other than sit, and allow your breath to guide you.

7. If, or when a thought pops into your mind, again, simply observe it.

8. Visualize your thoughts like clouds moving in a clear blue sky.

9. Say silently, "I am not my thoughts."

10. Say silently, "I observe my thoughts."

11. Say silently, "I'm not judgmental of my thoughts.

12. Say silently, "I can release my thoughts like a cloud moving in the sky."

13. Say silently, "I release any thoughts that do not serve my well being.

14. When you are ready, bring your focus and awareness back to your body.

15. Slowly open your eyes.

16. *Take as much time as you need to transition out of your meditation.*

As I said, the mind needs rest, and it also needs to be emptied. Not by force, or an insistence to stop our thoughts, but to find time in our day to sit quietly, and experience ourselves in the "being" rather than in the "doing."

The Zen Master Benkei Yotaku encapsulates this idea when he says, "Don't hate the arising of thoughts or stop thoughts that do arise. Simply realize that our original mind, right from the start is beyond thought, so that no matter what, you never get involved with thoughts. Illuminate original mind, and no other understanding is necessary."

*Note to self:*

*My thoughts come and go*
*I am not my thoughts*
*I am not attached to my thoughts*
*I am free of my thoughts*

# CHAPTER 13

# Desire

*Everyone has been made for some particular work, and
the desire for that work has been put in every heart.*
—*Rumi*

*Always desire to learn something useful.*
—*Sophocles*

Desire is having a want or longing for something that
can satisfy us, like food, or some type of pleasure, like
sex. Those kinds of things make us happy, so in essence,
we desire happiness. Our desires are for the most part syn-
onymous with our needs, and whatever we feel will fulfill

those needs, we make sure to provide them for ourselves, or gladly let others give to us.

But according to Buddha, we should; "Live joyfully, without desire." Well, we know that's hard to do, if not impossible, because we perceive desire as joy, and if you take that out of the equation, there doesn't seem like much to look forward to, or maybe even live for.

### *Without desire, what will motivate us, and what is it that we will wish for or aim for?*

It seems that we need desire just as much as desire needs us to need it. It's a vital part of our being. It motivates us and makes us passionate, and brings us the happiness that feels like the perfect antidote for overcoming the inevitable suffering we will experience in this lifetime. However, also according to Buddha, desire causes suffering because of our constant need for it. So that can make desire problematic, which means it's up to us to figure out what to do with this thing that churns in us daily, making us long for all sorts of things to keep ourselves satisfied.

From a Mindfulness perspective, it's important to be present with, and aware of what we desire, and know exactly what we want or are longing for, and why.

Yes, we can know that we're hungry, and feel an urge to satisfy our hunger, but by going deeper in our awareness, we may find that our hunger is more than just a desire for food, or sex, or whatever we think will satisfy us, and what we truly long for is something our heart and soul needs, which food, sex or whatever we're reaching out for cannot fulfill.

Desire is a natural thing to feel, and we cannot deny it, but we must keep in mind that there is much more in us that needs satisfying than can be realized by only sating the body. Satisfying our bodily desires is natural, but when we are not present, or mindful, it's easy to interpret the signals of the body as something we must give into right away, which is why we reach for things like food, sex, drugs or alcohol so quickly, thinking that's what our body is screaming out for, but really what we want and need is connection, understanding, and love. We are just unaware of it, which is why developing Mindfulness is so important.

By being fully present with our desire, and having a total awareness of what it is that we want, we won't give into our impulses quickly without pausing first to know why we feel we need that desire satisfied. We can even take in a deep breath so that we may get centered, go deeper within, which I encourage you to do as often as you can, and ask for a deeper understanding of what that desire is, and whether or not it is good for you, and if it is, what is the best way to serve it.

It's natural to want to satisfy a desire we have, or give into it, thinking it will make us feel better, which we naturally want to do for ourselves. Yes, we want to make ourselves feel as good as we possibly can, and that's totally understandable, but sometimes there are more mindful ways to satisfy what we want, and by not always reaching out for what's easy or immediate, which might not always be the best thing for us, we are so glad that we took the time to discover what that is.

Just like what we do with a baby when it cries, we immediately want to soothe it by giving it a breast or a pacifier, and that might be the very thing the baby needs. Yes, the baby may be hungry, but what it needs more than anything is a connection with the mother, and to know that it is loved and safe. I believe that is our greatest desire, and it begins when we are babies, and continues on in the life cycle.

Connection and love are our truest, deepest desires, and when we feel that we are not experiencing them, our body cries out in desperation to help us, because it's really our heart that's starving, and that's what we must learn to satisfy: our heart.

That's why connecting, first and foremost to ourselves, whether it be through meditation, or having some time in your day to get quiet and go within, and take what I call your *spiritual pulse*, you can know exactly what is churning inside your heart, and why. We cannot know what we want if we don't explore who we are, or what our deepest desires are. That means we must go inside to what I have called the house of self, and spend quiet, quality time with our "spiritual being", and ask it what it truly wants, and *listen*. Maybe it will tell you that what it longs for is to be loved and cared for, or listened to and understood, or maybe it will tell you that you can no longer live falsely, and that it's time to be who you really are, your authentic self, which you are not living out.

We owe it to ourselves to find out what our deepest desires are, and that means the ones that go way beyond the obvious, or first layer desires, like hunger for food or pleasure. There are much deeper desires in us, and sometimes we are unaware of what they are because we've been afraid to go further within to find out. But that is where we can hear the true longing in our heart, and where we can find out what it is we need to be providing for ourselves, before we try to satisfy anyone else.

**Desire, when coupled with meaning or purpose, can be our greatest realization in understanding what we're doing here.**

Having a desire to do something important, or to be in service for a cause that can help others, is a benevolent desire to have, and can be quite selfless and satisfying. When we feel the need to do something, not just for ourselves, but for others, that is when desire is no longer having a need to only satisfy us, but a need to satisfy and fulfill others, and our motivation to do that gives us an opportunity to realize a greater type of happiness than we've ever imagined.

We must understand our desires, and find out more about what they are telling us, and by doing so, we can discover more about ourselves. We may be pleasantly surprised to find out that our desires are driven by nothing more than love, and the need to share that love with others. When we listen to the desire of our heart, it will always tell us what we need to know, and from there, we can decide how we want to live out our desires in the best way possible.

# *Meditation for Connecting to Desire*

1.  Sit somewhere quiet.

2.  Close your eyes.

3.  Be aware of any sounds, feelings, thoughts or sensations you may be feeling in your body. Simply observe them.

4.  Put your focus and awareness onto your breath.

5.  Take a few deep breaths in and out.

6.  If at any time your mind begins to wander, bring your awareness and focus back to your breath.

7.  Say silently, "I desire."

8.  Say silently, "I desire love, peace, and understanding."

9.  Say silently, "How can I best serve my desire?"

10. Say silently, "Let my desire serve a greater good."

11. Bring your awareness back to your body.

12. When you are ready slowly open your eyes.

13. *Take the time you need to transition out of the meditation.*

## Note to self:

*I desire what is best for me*
*I desire what is best for others*
*I desire what is best for all*

# CHAPTER 14

## Emotions

*Flowers are restful to look at.*
*They have neither emotions nor conflicts.*
*—Sigmund Freud*

Part of our "human experience" is to feel things, and it runs the gamut from tremendous joy to deep suffering. Our heart can get touched one moment, and then hurt badly the very next. If we allow ourselves to stay open to the "slings and arrows of outrageous fortune, or to take arms against a sea of troubles" as Shakespeare said, then we are fully in life, embracing and handling all of the moments it presents to us, joyous and painful, and letting ourselves feel everything, fully and completely.

If we back away from life, and choose only to be open or receptive to it when it brings us joy and happiness, or those magic moments I spoke about in Chapter 2 (This Magic Moment), we are thwarting some of our deeper emotions, and that's like having an orchestra with only soft wind instruments, and not the deeper tones of a bass or cello, or listening to an opera with only soprano singers and no baritones, which wouldn't be the complete musical vocal range accompanying a well rounded drama. Life has all the notes, some high, some low, and our emotions reflect that. If you take any of them away, it's like having keys missing on a piano, or colors missing from a Crayola box. What kind of composition can you create with keys missing, and what kind of picture can you draw with missing colors?

There used to be a word to describe sadness, and it was called melancholy. I can't remember the last time I heard it. I guess depression took its place, but even that word seems like it's on its way out. It's as if we're living in a time where feeling sad or down, and anything below the "okay" line on the emotion measuring cup isn't in vogue or acceptable, and covering up the pain with pills or alcohol continues to be the tried and true solution.

But what's so disturbing about the rise in covering up our deep-seeded sadness, which could be a universal malaise from how disconnected we've become from ourselves and one another, is now we're facing an alarming addiction to opioids, which are synthetic drugs with narcotic properties. You feel pain, take a pill for it, and, yes, it may kill the pain—hence the name, "painkiller"—but you stand a greater chance of it killing you too, and people seem to be dropping like flies.

*Letting go of our suffering is the hardest work we will ever do.*
*—Buddha*

We know there's suffering, that's a given. But it's how hard we're willing to work through the pain that determines whether or not we can let go and transform it. And that's where we can step away from life, and ultimately give up. Some of us just don't want to work that hard, not even to help ourselves through our pain. So, we reach out. Not for help, but a drug, or a drink, and the very thing we should be reaching out for; human contact, is what we avoid, but need the most.

If you're suffering, you need to know that you are not alone, even though you may feel that you are. There is help out there, and it will find you because you are asking for it, even if you can't speak your pain out loud. What you ask for, even if you are screaming it silently to yourself, is your heart's deepest desire, and it is telling you that you need your pain healed, which is the greatest desire we can have: to heal our aching heart. And even if we ask for help in a silent prayer, and may not be ready, or afraid to say it to someone, we are desperately asking for our prayer to be heard. That is our deepest desire, to have the longing in our soul, heard, even if we don't always know that consciously. Or, it might be that we don't want help, and don't care to pray for it, but even so, there is always something in our "spiritual being", our higher consciousness that knows the pain and woes of our suffering. In spite of what we want, there is something bigger than us, be it God, divine consciousness, source, or whatever you want to call it, that is always present, and it moves through our spiritual being to help guide us.

If we allow ourselves to be taken over by the wear and tear of our human experiences, and not do the work I've explained to nurture our spirit through the practice of Mindfulness, we become disconnected from it. But even so, it waits silently, and patiently by our side, and listens to what we ask for. For some, they ask for nothing, and for others, they ask to be taken out of their misery. Many have asked for their bodies to be taken, for the pain has been too great for them to endure. It saddens me deeply when I think of all those fellow travelers on this miraculous life journey we are on who decided that the pain was just too much to bear, and excused themselves from continuing on with the rest of us.

For those of you that might feel this way, we want you here. I want you here, and am speaking for your loved ones that they want you here. You matter, and you deserve to live. What you are feeling are your emotions, which are, as I said, like notes on a piano, or the colors in the Crayola box, and they are different, and varied, and high and low, and dark and light, and unique just like you. Please hear me, you are a part of the "oneness" I've spoken about, and we're heading there together. Hang in there, and you will make it there with the rest of us. Each and every one of us can get to the "land of oneness" if we want to, and that should be your greatest desire, to realize your wholeness, your most authentic self, and continue on this difficult, but extraordinary journey called life, as we make our way to this sacred land of peace, harmony, and unconditional love. Yes, it exists, but you'll have to wait to find out where it is.

Remember, you are a "spiritual being having a human experience", and there can be enormous amounts of suffering being human, as Buddha reminds us. But you can do this, you really can! Tell yourself this is true, and it will become the core belief you live by daily. Let it be your affirmation, your mantra; "I can do this!"

If you happen to be suffering, try and tell someone about the pain that is in your heart, and do whatever you can to have your emotional needs met. Yes, our emotions have needs, and they need to be heard, understood, and cared for. If you're feeling something like sadness, allow yourself to feel it (do not push it away, or reach for something to numb it), but instead, ask your sadness what it needs.

I advise in my book, *Says Who?*, "Behind every emotion is a thought, and our thoughts are trying to tell us something." If we listen to them, they will tell us what they want us to know, which might be to love ourselves better, or to stop beating ourselves up by being so critical, and saying such cruel and mean things. That is why it's so important to work with our thoughts, and change them into ones that can serve our well being in the best way possible.

Each of us will have a dark night of the soul at some point in our lives, maybe many of them, which is like having an "***emotional fever.***" That means that one of our emotions needs special attention and care, and if we viewed our emotions, as I said, as having needs, we would take care of whichever emotion needs the most help, just like we would a sore throat or a cold. Neglecting what ails us only makes it get worse, and same is said for not being nurturing of an emotion that needs our love and support.

At one point we must ask ourselves how have we fallen this low in our despair? What is happening to us? Not just each of us individually, but collectively. The world is suffering, and by that, I mean, the entire planet—Mother Nature, and so many of her inhabitants. That is why tending to our own emotions, and the pain and suffering we're experiencing is so important, because we are not only healing our own souls, but also healing the *Anima Mundi*, which is Latin for "the soul of the world." This means there is an "intrinsic connection between all living things on the planet" and, as I've said a few times before, "What you do with your today, and what I do with my today, affects everyone's today on the planet."

We are part of the **Collective Consciousness**, which means there is a "unifying force that we all share." And something that we all share and have in common is an array of emotions. All of them are like the perfect notes in the symphony of life. We mustn't tamper, thwart, numb, deny, or kill any single one of our emotions because they are our soul's music, and all we need to do is to understand them better.

In the following Kahlil Gibran poem, *Song of the Soul*, he writes about the deep emotions that stir his heart:

### Song of the Soul
*In the depth of my soul there is*
*A wordless song—a song that lives*
*In the seed of my heart.*

*It refuses to melt with ink on*
*Parchment; it engulfs my affection*
*In a transparent cloak and flows,*
*But not upon my lips.*

*How can I sing it? I fear it may*
*Mingle with earthly ether;*
*To whom shall I sing it? It dwells*
*In the house of my soul, in fear of*
*Harsh ears.*

*When I look into my inner eyes*
*I see the shadow of its shadow;*
*When I touch my fingertips*
*I feel its vibrations.*
*The deeds of my hands heed its*
*Presence as a lake must reflect*
*The glittering stars;*
*My tears reveal it, as bright drops of dew*
*Reveal the secret of a withering rose.*

*It is a song composed by contemplation,*
*And published by silence,*
*And shunned by clamor,*
*And folded by truth,*
*And repeated by dreams,*
*And understood by love,*
*And hidden by awakening,*
*And sung by the soul.*

*It is the song of love;*
*What Cain or Esau could sing it?*
*It is more fragrant than jasmine;*
*What voice could enslave it?*
*It is heartbound, as a virgin's secret;*
*What string could quiver it?*
*Who dares unite the roar of the sea*
*And the singing of the nightingale?*
*Who dares compare the shrieking tempest*
*To the sigh of an infant?*
*Who dares speak aloud the words*
*Intended for the heart to speak?*
*What human dares sing in voice*
*The song of God?*

So, what are you waiting for? Stop numbing yourself, and start feeling more. That's right; feel even more than you do. That's what being alive is about—to feel it all! It's okay to feel both the highs and lows, and if you feel it's too much to be gripped with emotions like sadness, fear or anger, remember what I said in Chapter 4 (The Present): "*You are the surfer. Ease into the wave.*" You can do this. You really can, and if you **think** you can't, remember you are creating those thoughts and beliefs in your mind, and can change them if you want at any time.

Let yourself hear the "song of your soul" which has every single musical note in it, both high and low, and don't be afraid to share it. Be proud of your emotional range, and unafraid to be completely present in your aliveness.

Celebrate your happiness, and gently tend to your sadness, or any emotion that shows signs of hopelessness or malaise. Don't wait until one of them has spiked a fever, and you've allowed it to infect you with despondency. Be diligent in practicing Mindfulness, and allow yourself to be fully present in every single emotion you are feeling, even if it's difficult or painful. Don't escape the dark night of your soul by doing the worst possible thing you could, which is drowning it, or exacerbating it with drugs or alcohol. That really is anathema to a troubled emotion, and I can only best describe it as rubbing a wound in salt, or even worse, putting gasoline on a fire. Your emotions need one thing, and one thing only, to be felt, nurtured and loved. And you owe it to yourself to give your emotions what they need. All they ask of you is to understand them, and have compassion for them. And that means with acceptance, non-judgment and love, which is the cherry on top of Mindfulness—being in the present moment with acceptance, non-judgment and love.

And if, at any time, you feel sadness or deep despair, and feel like you want to give up, promise me that you will at least try this: Put your hand on your heart and silently say, "Find me light, I am ready for you to shine your warmth on me, and embrace me with unconditional love." And you will see that the darkness will eventually move past you, and become a thing of yesterday. And like all the other things that pained you and did not serve you well, they will no longer exist, and you can change the memory of them to a present one, as I spoke about in Chapter 3 (The Past).

As I continue to say throughout the book, this present moment is the moment that matters the most because you are in it, and if you value being alive, then you value the moment you are most alive in, which is right now, and that means also valuing the emotions you are having. You can move through the darkness because it is not permanent.

As the Greek philosopher Haraclitus said, "Change is the only constant in life." Everything changes, including our pain. If you can believe that, you will not be at the effect of whatever emotions you are feeling, but instead experience them, and be present for what they have to teach you. Because remember: some of the hardest moments of our lives can be our greatest teachers. They can have important and valuable lessons for us to learn from, and once we get what it is, we can then let the moment go, and our pain with it.

And more importantly, no matter what difficulty or pain you're experiencing, never stop asking your "spiritual being" to pull you up, and help you move through whatever challenges or hardships you are facing. You may not know this, but **you already are that spiritual being** that is always trying to make its presence known in your human body, but we don't always pay attention to it because we're too busy trying to have so many successful human experiences by running and going, and doing and competing, that we don't value our spirituality, which might want us to rest and reflect, and not try so hard all the time to be "something or someone" other than who we truly are. Sometimes it takes a life-altering incident to remind us of that, but don't wait for the possibility of that to happen for you to realize this. All that our spiritual being wants is for us to realize our true nature, our wholeness, our most authentic self. Ask for it, and it will show it to you in so many beautiful ways.

# Meditation for Emotions

1. Sit somewhere quiet.

2. Close your eyes gently.

3. Be aware of any sounds, thoughts, feelings or sensations in your body. Simply observe them.

4. Put your focus and awareness onto your breath.

5. Take a few deep breaths in and out.

6. Say silently, "I am aware of my feelings."

7. Say silently, "My emotions matter to me."

8. Say silently, "I do not need to hide or deny what I am feeling."

9. Say silently to yourself, "I can handle what I'm feeling."

10. Say silently, "I will get through what I am feeling."

11. Say silently, "My spiritual being is always with me."

12. Bring your focus and awareness back to your body.

13. When you are ready open your eyes slowly.

14. *Take your time to transition out of your meditation.*

*Note to self:*

*I am alive*
*I feel myself*
*I celebrate my emotions*
*I listen to the song of my soul*
*I am unafraid to ask for help, or share what is in my*
*heart with others*

# CHAPTER 15

# Knowledge

*The good life is one inspired by love*
*and guided by knowledge.*
—*Bertrand Russell*

Confucius said, "Real knowledge is to know the extent of one's ignorance." But how do we know our ignorance if we don't see it about ourselves? Mindfulness keeps you in the moment with total awareness, and that means it shows you when you're lacking knowledge about something. It shines a bright light on that which you may not know so you can become better informed, and then act on it mindfully.

When we're present, and aware of who we are in the moment, we are also aware of when we are being inauthentic to ourselves. This is the brilliance of Mindfulness.

It provides a mirror for our soul to look into, and when we don't see a clear reflection, we look that much deeper to find it. And that is when we recognize that there is more for us to know, always. We never stop learning, and the path of self-realization is to keep peeling the onion, and lifting the veils of illusion so that we may see what is real, and by having the right knowledge, we will know what is real and what is not.

So where do we find this knowledge? Is it in books? Is it taught in schools? Do our leaders teach it to us, or our rabbis or priests? Or is it to be found on a mountaintop where we sit and chant with one who has devoted their life to meditation and non-materialism? Knowledge can be found in all of those places, but that does not mean that is where it ends.

**Knowledge is like an ever-flowing stream of water, and where you stop to drink from it, is where you will become quenched.**

Thirst is what is never-ending, and depending on what it is that keeps you wanting more, you will follow the stream no matter where it flows, and never lose sight of it even when it is hard to find. We must move with the river of knowledge, and go to great lengths to keep us properly hydrated with the correct facts and information.

Nature is the perfect analogy for knowledge because there is so much richness of information that exists in it, and when we examine nature closely, and see how it functions, we will learn everything we need to know. But out of ignorance, we look away from the things that show us what is most real, and choose instead to let greed and avarice replace the purest of knowledge, and that is when it is lost.

It is those that venture forward, and choose not to let ignorance steer them away from the wholeness within. They know that there is more work to be done to repair what is broken or damaged in all of us, so that a healing can happen not just for one, but for all. Remember what I said in Chapter 8 (Coexistence): "What you do with your today, and what I do with my today, will effect all of the todays of everyone on the planet."

Knowledge in the hands of a troubled soul who hasn't healed what is damaged or broken within them is how we get dictators or rulers who are dangerous, or even crazy, as I said in Chapter 11 (Perception). They are the ones that are ill equipped to be in power, and yet somehow, they do have one particular piece of knowledge, and that is how to misuse power. It's as if they've read every book and manual on how to manipulate power, and now they are in a position to show us how they have mastered the art of it. Only it is lies distorted as truth. That is why we must be the ones to know what *true knowledge* is so that we can defend ourselves from lies and deception, and see with our clearest of perception that the emperor, does, in fact, have no clothes.

Without having correct knowledge, it's easy for us to be fooled, especially by those who are experts on deception.

That saying, "wolf in sheep's clothing" means that there will always be someone who "seems to be good" but unless we have the depth of perception to see what is true and authentic, and know what is real and what is not, we will mistake something or someone that is not good at all, and believe otherwise. That is when deception can ignite the masses, which is what happened in Nazi Germany.

What is it that we have still to learn? That we are afraid to know ourselves, and fearful of what we may find out? That there is darkness there?

Of course, there is darkness there. There is darkness in everyone, and it is called the "shadow", and if we don't make it conscious to us, it will, as Jung said, "appear in our lives as fate." He also observed that, "It is a fact that cannot be denied: the wickedness of others becomes our own wickedness because it kindles something evil in our own hearts." Be aware of what kindles in your heart.

We must be unafraid to go towards the darkness within us, and shine a light on it, a very bright light. Without the knowledge of our darkness, we cannot have the true knowledge of who we are, and know the real meaning of life, and what we are doing here. If we are not willing to do that, we will rely on deception and false knowledge. We will settle for ignorance instead of true knowledge, and that will be enough to get by, but is that what it has come to for us? Have we really stooped even lower in our "human experience?"

We're living in a time when we have something called "fake news." If we don't know real news from fake news, then what's the difference really? And how can we know the difference between what's real or fake if we don't really even know who we are; the *authentic self?*

Our perception is being tested, which is why it's so very important to make sure you're seeing clearly. That means yourself first, and only then does your eyesight become 20/20, with a little bit of X-ray vision in there too.

It's time for us to be the superheroes we read about in comic books. They didn't mess around. They knew when evil was lurking, and they went after it with a vengeance. But we can't go after anything until we have the absolute correct knowledge of how to do that. This takes some careful planning, and learning from the mistakes we've made from our past.

We must be even wiser knowledge seekers now, and look even deeper for the most sacred truth, for truth is sacred, and we must honor it as such.

The saying that "Knowledge is power" is acknowledging that it is, in fact, powerful, but in the wrong hands, you have an inversion like how Hitler inverted the Swastika. Power without the knowledge that hate is the greatest lie of all, is the most dangerous power there is, and we must never forget that. Know the truth, and know it well, and when you are in the presence of anyone who says they have more knowledge than you, listen to what that is. If they are not espousing love, then they know very little, and it is your job to teach them what you know. Speak of your knowledge, and when they ask you how you came to know what you know, tell them that your heart was your greatest teacher.

# Meditation for Knowledge

1. Sit somewhere quiet.

2. Close your eyes.

3. Be aware of any sounds, feeling, thoughts or sensations in your body. Simply observe them.

4. Put your focus and awareness onto your breath.

5. Take a few deep breaths in and out.

6. Say silently, "Let me know true knowledge."

7. Say silently, "Let me be wise in what I choose to believe."

8. Say silently, "Let me not be led by false knowledge."

9. Say silently, "Let me shine my light on truth."

10. When you are ready, bring your focus and awareness back to your body.

11. Slowly open your eyes.

12. *Take as much time as you need before you transition out of your meditation.*

*Note to self:*

*I seek true knowledge*
*Knowledge of light*
*Knowledge of love*
*There is no other knowledge*

# CHAPTER 16

# **Behavior**

*Human behavior flows from three main sources:*
*desire, emotion, and knowledge.*
—*Plato*

When did bad behavior become acceptable? When did saying things that were mean and offensive become okay? When did insulting other's religion, sex, or gender become the "norm?"

I don't know about you, but it seems there was a time when people were nicer to one another, and I'm hoping that with Mindfulness seeping into the mainstream, people will find their way back to politeness and kindness by being present and aware of how they're behaving.

When I was young, you called your friend's parents "Mr. & Mrs.", but that does seem a little too formal today, and I would be the first to say to my children's friends, "You don't have to call me Mrs. Nadrich."

But, I also feel we've moved so far away from speaking to one another with respect, that when someone is genuinely polite and well-mannered, it almost takes me aback, and I find myself thinking, "They must be from somewhere else." And where could that be, Buckingham Palace?

I was surprised to find that there is an actual list of "the ten worst mannered cities" but not to my surprise, Los Angeles is on it. Don't get me wrong, I love my city, but people spend most of their time in their cars here, and when someone occasionally let's you go ahead of them in busy traffic, you automatically assume they either meditate or do yoga. When you practice Mindfulness, you're just more mindful, and you become more aware of when someone is indicating that they would like to go in front of you in traffic, or when you're walking in front of another person, you hold the door open for them, instead of letting it swing shut in their face.

Mindfulness not only makes you more aware in the present moment, but it also makes you aware when you're not the only person in it, and helps you think of how you can treat someone with kindness and compassion.

It becomes the way you behave in all of the moments you are in, or at least aspire to, and like in Taoism, a Chinese philosophy, you live in harmony with nature, and all that exists. When we practice Mindfulness, we are much more attuned to living in alignment with our authentic self. What that means essentially is that we're honoring our true nature, and therefore honoring and respecting the nature of all people and things, and that means Mother Nature too.

It's basically living life in balance. And when it's not, we feel it. You just know when something feels out of whack, but with the way people are treating each other lately, "out of whack" is getting harder to detect because it's become normalized, which is why being present and mindful is needed now more than ever.

There are many theories about human evolution, and if you hold the belief that we've evolved from apes, then for the most part we've done pretty well, and our behavior has improved significantly. But as of recently, with all the hate we're seeing playing out in the world, it seems that we've taken a giant step backwards and resorting more to our animal instincts, and as I discussed in Chapter 11 (Perception), if we stop caring about our fellow man, then it's back to the game of "survival of the fittest"—when we have moved as far away from compassion as we possibly can.

"Behavior is the mirror in which everyone shows their image", said Johann Wolfgang von Goethe, and what we're seeing reflecting back to us right now isn't such a pretty sight. Hate, racism, intolerance. Comparing these times to Nazi Germany, which shakes me to my core, having lost my father's entire family in the Holocaust, is deeply disturbing. It's as if we've done a time travel, not "back to the future", but way back to our past. Why anyone would want to relive the horrors of what happened then makes no sense at all. Unless, that is, we've fallen asleep, and we're in a deep slumber of unconsciousness, which can happen, has happened, and looks like it could happen again, if we're not careful.

How can we gauge how far man has fallen, if not by his behavior, and when should we have reason for genuine concern if not when the times that we live in are being compared to one that has been recorded as the darkest and most evil time ever in human history? When I think of Nazi Germany, I've asked myself many times, how could it have happened?" I know millions of people have asked that same question, but I have had this almost obsessive curiosity about what were people unaware of, or not seeing, or choosing not to see. And when do we know we've hit that threshold where not seeing what was there all along, is now too late to do anything about?

It reminds me of the final stanza in T.S Eliot's poem, The Hollow Men:

> *This is the way the world ends*
> *This is the way the world ends*
> *This is the way the world ends*
> *Not with a bang but a whimper.*

I think human behavior is the only way to gauge how far we've moved away from our humanity, and based on what we're seeing, or for those that are actually seeing it, we are moving farther away from decent behavior daily. So, what can we do about it before it's too late? How can my today of awareness become your today of awareness, and my today of compassion become your today of compassion? How can what I do be that ripple in the ocean that reverberates out wide and far? I have to trust that my awakening will inspire others to awaken, and anyone who is more awake than me, I will aspire to be like them.

We can begin by practicing Mindfulness every moment of each day, and it will help us stay awake and aware when we even begin to step out of the moment of caring about one another.

Let someone go in front of you in traffic; look behind you to see if anyone needs the door held open for them. And don't stop there. Think of other ways you can change how you act or conduct yourself towards others. Set your intentions in the morning to go out in your day and be truly caring and mindful, even if someone is not treating you in the same way. Don't take their tone, or mimic their thoughtlessness, but instead go more out of your way to be kind. This is the *"raise your consciousness challenge"* I talked about it in Chapter 9 (Consciousness), which is being a more evolved human being on the planet. Are you going to take it? I really hope so because now is the time to do it, and as the rabbinic sage Hillel the Elder famously said, "If I am not for myself, who will be for me? If I am only for myself, what am I? If not now, when?"

# Meditation for Behavior

1.  Sit somewhere quiet.

2.  Close your eyes.

3.  Be aware of any sounds, thoughts, feelings, or sensations in your body. Simply observe them.

4.  Put your focus and awareness onto your breath.

5.  Take a few deep breaths in and out.

6.  Say silently, "Let me be aware of my behavior."

7.  Say silently, "Let my behavior be mindful."

8.  Say silently, "Let my behavior not hurt or offend others."

9.  Say silently, "Let my behavior reflect my authentic self."

10. When you are ready bring your focus and awareness back to your body.

11. Slowly open your eyes.

12. *Transition out of your meditation when you are ready.*

***Note to self:***

*My behavior reflects the best of who I am*
*I can make a difference by my behavior*
*Let my behavior be a light for others*

# PART III

## Living

*We love life, not because we are used to living but because we are used to loving.*
*—Friedrich Nietzsche*

*Open your eyes, look within.*
*Are you satisfied with the life you're living?*
*—Bob Marley*

# CHAPTER 17

# Love

*Love conquers all.*
*—Latin phrase from Eclogue X by Virgil*

Mother Teresa said; "Let us always meet each other with a smile, for the smile is the beginning of love." I think we could be smiling a lot more at one another, and I feel it's time to seriously rethink love because it seems that we've either forgotten how to do it, or our standards for how well we can has dropped significantly.

When I see what's going on in the world, be it the political chaos, violence, or insanity, if you want to really call it out, I always think to myself, "love is nowhere in sight." It's just not here. Nowhere even near. It's gone, bye-bye. "In a galaxy far, far away." Wait a minute, that's from a movie! And it's called Star Wars. And it's all about good vs. evil. We watched those movies and thought they were great, but have we learned nothing about what they showed and taught us that when love is taken over by man's evil drive for power, it goes missing, and it seems that it's missing more each day. It is up to us to find it again, and remember that it is our sole purpose here: to love.

What else is there really? We may think we want "this and that", and as I described in Chapter 13 (Desire), "Believe we need to cater to our more basic cravings and longings without knowing the greater desires we can fulfill, not just for ourselves, but for the greater good of all." And that's because we're not delving deeper into ourselves, and looking closely at our hearts, and listening to our "soul song" to find out what it's telling us. The Beatles were right, "Love is all you need." And that's all we need to know above anything else. Without that most simple, yet most wise piece of knowledge, it doesn't matter what else we come to know, because without knowing that, we know nothing.

Love should be our morning cup of wisdom, and "I love you" should be what we tell each other, each and every day before we say "good-morning."

If love is not what sends you out in your day, you will feel something missing, and not know quite what it is. It will gnaw at you, and make you feel grumpy, and you'll approach everything a little less nice. You'll sense that something doesn't feel right, and so will others about you, but until you realize that you forgot to turn the love light on in your heart, your day, and all of your days will be less bright because of it, and will stay that way until you remember to switch it on.

Love is the super glue that keeps our wholeness together, and when we don't nurture it, that is when we can become broken; if for no other reason that when something isn't held together well, it stands a greater chance of becoming damaged.

Protecting our wholeness should be paramount, especially knowing that it protects our ability to love. Why would we want to damage the very thing that keeps us open, kind and generous, which is love, but also risk the possibility of destroying our ability to feel it? We don't realize how we are actually killing off a part of ourselves when we shut down to love. But that's not to say that even the most hardened heart can't be softened by using the very thing that it has kept away from itself out of fear, and that's love.

Yes, fear is what pushes love away. But it's really the fear of feeling love and being vulnerable that keeps it at a distance. If you don't allow yourself to feel the range of emotions I spoke about it in Chapter 14 (Emotions), then you will fear love because it's too painful for you to feel how much your heart longs for it. So, what do you do? You deny it, or cut it off in you. And that's like wrapping a tourniquet around your heart, and stopping the blood supply to your body. Poor heart. All it wants to do is to love.

And yet, even in the presence of someone who has shut down their heart to such a degree that it seems that love was never there, love can be found again, amidst the debris of their personal wreckage, and we must never give up, not only on our own hardened heart, but someone else's.

If we revisit Carl Sagan's quote, "We are a way for the cosmos to know itself," then the cosmos is having a field day knowing that what we're doing on this planet is to learn about love, and hopefully we'll get it right before we destroy it.

I believe that we can transform anything, especially hate into love, but we've got to not only change the negative and hateful thoughts we breed in our minds, but also practice Mindfulness in all areas of our lives.

That means we are committed to staying awake and aware at all times, and making love our number one priority to be mindful about. If even for one moment, we step away from protecting it, nurturing it, practicing it, and encouraging it in others, let there be a loud bell go off in our head, and we immediately stand to attention.

**Be present about love. Make it your purpose, and then declare your intentions from there.**

You will know what you are supposed to do with your life if you always make love your guide.

And use your voice in the name of love. Speak up when you see that it is missing, like a child that's been kidnapped, and speak out against anyone that tries to kill it off, and call them a murderer.

This brings to mind W.H. Auden's, love poem for humanity, "September 1, 1939" which he wrote during the outbreak of World War II. Here is a stanza with the famous line; "We must love one another or die."

LOVE

*All I have is a voice*
*To undo the folded lie,*
*The romantic lie in the brain*
*Of the sensual man-in-the-street*
*And the lie of Authority*
*Whose buildings grope the sky:*
*There is no such thing as the State,*
*And no one exists alone;*
*Hunger allows no choice*
*To the citizen or the police;*
*We must love one another or die.*

# Meditation for Love

1. Sit somewhere quiet.

2. Close your eyes.

3. Be aware of any sounds, thoughts, feelings, or sensations in your body. Simply observe them.

4. Put your focus and awareness on your breath.

5. Take a few deep breaths in and out.

6. If at any time your mind begins to wander, bring your focus and awareness back to your breath.

7. Say silently, "Love is in my heart."

8. Say silently, "I choose love always."

9. Repeat this as many times as you want.

10. When you feel ready, bring your focus and awareness back to your body sitting in meditation.

11. Slowly open your eyes.

12. *At your own pace, transition out of the meditation.*

## *Note to self:*

*Love is truth*
*Love is all there is*
*Love now*

# CHAPTER 18

# Acceptance

*Happiness can exist only in acceptance.*
*—George Orwell*

"I like you, do you like me?"
Isn't that how children approach one another, with total openness and acceptance? They have this pure, innocent way of expressing themselves, and have a completely disarming attitude like, "Hey, I want you to be my friend." Kids don't even make each other earn it. They make up their minds pretty quickly that they like you, and before you know it, they've put their arm around you and declared you their best friend. It doesn't matter what color skin you

have, your religion, or if you don't identify as any particular gender.

Children don't pick you as their friend based on any of that. They like you because it's natural for them to, until they've been brainwashed to hate, and everything changes after that.

I remember when I was twelve years old, and at my best friend's house having dinner with her family. I sat there and wondered why they seemed cold and unfriendly. I sensed that something wasn't right, but I wasn't sure what it was. A few days later, I was on the phone with her making plans to get together again, and her brother came on the phone. He asked me if I knew what a "wej" was, and I said no. He laughed, and said, "That's a Jew spelled backwards." That's what I was, a "wej." He laughed again and started to make fun of me by repeating over and over again, "Ora is a wej, Ora is a wej".

I felt my heart sink, as if someone had knocked the wind out of me. It was my first experience with anti-Semitism, and it was the most hurtful thing I had ever felt. From that moment onward, I knew I was different than my best friend and her family, who were Roman Catholic, and that I wasn't accepted by them, even though she and I loved each other because that's all we knew, and that's what felt most true to us—we were being authentic to what was true in our hearts. The knowledge of her family's non-acceptance of me was devastating, but it taught me the biggest lesson of my life, that prejudice exists, and it's closer to home than we can imagine.

We are not born to hate. We're not hard wired like that. We learn how to hate, and not to accept someone based on their religion, sex, gender, color of skin, or anything that marks us as different from one another.

As quickly as a child decides to like someone, we, as adults, are as quick not to accept anyone who is different than us, and it takes us less than a minute to dismiss or reject someone who we view as inferior because they don't look, think or act like we do. It's okay if you feel that someone isn't your cup of tea, but that doesn't mean you have to view them as a threat or an enemy, which some people do with anyone who's different than them. They just can't find a place to file them away in their mind, so it's easier to put them in the dislike or hate category.

If it's our differences that threaten us, then it's acceptance that can dissipate the fear of dissimilarity.

What is unfamiliar to us can seem threatening, but if we can approach one another with an openness to get to know who we are in spite of our differences, and take a genuine interest in discovering what it is that makes us unique, then acceptance becomes a genuine power, and those that can practice it become the empowered.

### *He who accepts love in his heart is truly powerful.*

There are people like Martin Luther King Jr. who refused to give into the belief that hatred was more powerful than love, and devoted their life to dispelling it. "I refuse to accept the view," he famously said, "that mankind is so tragically bound to the starless midnight of racism and war that the bright daybreak of peace and brotherhood can never become a reality... I believe that unarmed truth and unconditional love will have the final word."

Refusing to accept the view that "mankind is so tragically bound to the starless midnight of racism and war" is standing up to intolerance, because it's not letting the limitations of those who are not connected to their wholeness, speak for all of humanity, and certainly not the humanity we hold in our own hearts, which is not bound by hatred, and does feel acceptance towards others. We have to be able to say, "enough" when it comes to hatred, and the only way to do that is by not letting it become our reality, but instead, always steering hatred towards "unconditional love" and know, as Martin Luther King Jr. said, "it will have the final word."

As I said in Chapter 16 (Behavior), "Think of other ways you can change how you act or conduct yourself towards others. Set your intentions in the morning to go out in your day and be truly caring and mindful, and even if someone is not treating you in the same way, don't take their tone, or mimic their thoughtlessness, but instead go more out of your way to be kind. This is the *raise your consciousness challenge.*"

Acceptance raises the consciousness bar high, and when we bring others into our hearts, even if they seem unfamiliar or foreign to us, we are functioning from our higher self; our spiritual being, and we know that oneness is the ultimate "unarmed truth."

We are one, but we have split apart into billions of people all over the world, and by each and every one of us holding love in our hearts, and living with acceptance of all people that walk this earth with us, no matter their skin color, religion, gender, or any differences we may have, we will find our way back to the *land of oneness* that I've spoken about, and realize that it's right here where we are. But we've moved far away from it. We have forgotten this truth in our slumber of unconsciousness, and must awaken to it so that we can return to our conscious homeland. But we must realize that we have not seen clearly for a very long time; that our perception has been distorted, and must now see through a lens of acceptance of one another.

Mindfulness will help us return to our conscious homeland. It reminds us that we are here in this moment of "now" and that there is no other moment than this one, and all that this moment asks us to do is to feel love and acceptance in our hearts; towards ourselves, and others.

That's what all the moments of our lives ask of us. Is that so very hard? Is that not possible for us to do? Ask yourself how you inhabit your moments. Are you awake and aware, and able to see the beauty in your fellow man, or do you perceive them with judgment and hate? Take off those distorted glasses, and see through eyes of "unarmed truth." There is no clearer vision you will have than seeing through the lens of love and acceptance, and what you will see will open your heart so wide, you will know that this is the truest vision of all, and never want to cover your eyes, or turn away from love again.

# Meditation for Acceptance

1. Sit somewhere quiet.

2. Close your eyes.

3. Be aware of any sounds, thoughts, feelings, or sensations you may be experiencing in your body. Simply observe them.

4. Put your focus and awareness on your breath.

5. Take a few deep breaths in and out.

6. If at any time your mind begins to wander, simply bring your awareness back to your breath.

7. Say silently, "I accept myself."

8. Say silently, "I accept all beings."

9. Say silently, "May love and acceptance always guide me."

10. When you're ready, bring your focus and awareness back to your body sitting in meditation.

11. Slowly open your eyes.

12. *At your own pace, transition out of the meditation.*

*Note to self:*

*I accept myself*
*I accept others*
*Acceptance is my truth*

# CHAPTER 19

## Truth

*The truth shall set you free.*
*—John 8:32*

Here are some of my truths: I am alive. I feel love in my heart. I want goodness for the world. I am saddened by hatred. I believe that light will overcome darkness. What are some of your truths? Close your eyes and see what comes to mind.

Truth is like cream, and it will always rise to the top. It's what you keep adding on top of it that will determine if it weighs it down, cause it to change color, or alter its sweetness. What is your cup filled with?

Truth can be exciting, invigorating, uplifting, inspiring, disappointing, devastating, and very hard to take. So much so that we can keep pushing it away, and pretend that truth is something other than what it is, which makes it a lie, and convince ourselves that the lie is truth, and convince others too. There's that inversion theory, like the Swastika. Make something other than what it was intended to be, and the results can be catastrophic.

But a lie can only exist for as long as it is believed to be true, but eventually, truth is always revealed; like the old man standing behind the curtain in The Wizard of Oz.

Who would have thought that the scary wizard who had Dorothy, The Tin Man, The Cowardly Lion, and the Scarecrow so afraid of, was really an old, little man orchestrating everything behind a curtain. It took Dorothy's dog Toto to figure it out, and the "spell of the wizard was broken." What spell are we living under? What lies are we believing? And who is the wizard that is telling us something that isn't true? If we use the yellow brick road in The Wizard of Oz as a metaphor for our life's journey, then we must know that we will come across many lies along the long and winding road. And if we choose to believe them, then the wizard gets to keep on pulling the strings, whoever that is in our life that we've given power to, and we will remain scared and fearful of them.

Thank God for Toto. He was one smart dog. There's no fooling dogs. They can smell a liar better than we can sometimes. But why wait for someone else to pull back the curtain? Why be afraid to see the lie for what it is, and do whatever we can to reveal the truth. Truth has a way of making it known. It might take a while, and cause a lot of confusion and chaos because it's not being seen or acted on. But in the wake of whatever its absence causes, we can only hope whatever it caused by our denying of it, we will be able to recover from it.

If you really want to be a part of the raise your consciousness challenge I spoke about in Chapter 9 (Consciousness), then seeing and speaking the truth have to be your absolute top priorities. There's no hope of raising our consciousness if we won't go to great measures to make sure that a lie has been revealed, and truth is put back in its place. But we must decide what we're willing to do to make that happen, and that is where Mindfulness will always help us do it.

Being present and aware keeps us honest. It makes us see what is really going on in the moment we are in, and even if we want to turn away from it, we can't because our awareness of the truth is so heightened.

It's very hard to lie to yourself when you are in a state of Mindfulness because you are facing what you're experiencing with openness and acceptance. Yes, you may feel uncomfortable, and may not like that you're up close and personal with something that is difficult or challenging, but you know if it comes down to having to choose between a lie or truth, you cannot but surrender to what you are conscious of.

Your awareness is your consciousness, and you either choose to act on it or you don't, and what you are left with is the knowing that you could or could not rise to your higher self.

Remember what I said in Chapter 9 (Consciousness): "You can only function from a level of awareness that you are on, and if that level is low, you will operate from a lower, or baser level of consciousness, and if you act from a higher level, it is the consciousness of your higher self that is present."

Higher consciousness is a state of "elevated awareness" and we can only realize that when we are present and awake, which is being in a state of Mindfulness.

Be in the "here and now" of truth. Know with certainty what is it that you are seeing. And even if you're just having a hunch, and that hunch is telling you something beyond what's on the surface, follow it and see where it leads you. You may be led to the biggest lie imaginable, and by you following your gut, not turning away from what you were sensing, you could be the very person that can discover a lie so serious, that it took *you* to pull back the curtain, and reveal that there is nothing to be afraid of anymore because the lie has been exposed for what it is.

Here's a truth for us to see without our rose-colored glasses: There is no wizard. We just want to believe that there is. And why do we need to believe something that isn't true? Who is it that we need to tell us who we are, and what we should do, and what we should believe? Do you need that?

Do you need to have a wizard in your life, or do *you* want to be the wizard, living in your own "Land of Oz", walking your own yellow brick road? It may be long and it may be winding, but let truth guide you on it every step of the way. And when you get to the top of it—the Emerald City—you will find at the center of it the Royal Palace of Oz, where the throne room is. And who do you think you will find there? You will find yourself. That will be your greatest truth; that you ended up finding out who you really are, and you were brave enough to reveal the lies along the way.

Be a **truth traveller**, a **lie exposer**, and above all, a **consciousness raiser**. Truth raises consciousness, and without your "spiritual being" always striving to transcend this "human experience", truth cannot prevail. Trust in your heart, and as Martin Luther King Jr. said;  know "that unarmed truth and unconditional love will have the final word."

# *Meditation for Truth*

1. Sit somewhere quiet.

2. Close your eyes.

3. Be aware of any sounds, thoughts, feelings or sensations in your body. Simply observe them.

4. Bring your awareness and focus to your breath.

5. Take a few deep breaths in and out.

6. Say silently, "I seek truth."

7. Say silently, "Let me be guided by truth."

8. Say silently, "Let me be in service to truth."

9. When you are ready, bring your awareness back to your body.

10. Slowly open your eyes.

11. *Take as much time as you need to transition out of your meditation.*

### *Note to self:*

*I honor truth*
*I practice truth*
*I live truth*

# CHAPTER 20

# **Honesty**

*Honesty is the first chapter in the book of wisdom.*
*—Thomas Jefferson*

*Treat those who are good with goodness, and also treat*
*those who are not good with goodness. Thus goodness is*
*attained. Be honest to those who are honest, and be also*
*honest to those who are not honest.*
*Thus honesty is attained.*
*—Lao Tzu*

As we peel away the onion on the path of self-realization, and lift the veils of the inauthentic self, we will invariably face truths about ourselves that might not be so easy to accept. But we must do it in order to know who we really are, and what we're made of. Yes, we're made of "star stuff", and that means we're heavenly beings, but we don't usually live our lives thinking of ourselves as having heavenly or divine qualities, which we do. We are so busy having a "human experience" and telling ourselves all sorts of things about what we think we are, or who we think we have to be in order to be loved and accepted, that our inner dialogue doesn't always support our true nature, which can cause us to live dishonestly.

Mindfulness keeps you living honestly because you're present with exactly what you're thinking, feeling, and experiencing, and no matter what that is, you accept it with non-judgment.

It doesn't let you off the hook, not in a burdensome way, but in a purely helpful way. It supports you being present and honest so you can protect yourself from slipping out of self-awareness because you know how counterproductive that can be to living authentically.

We live authentically when the path we choose through life is congruent or harmonious with who we really are, and when we function as who we really are there is a plethora of benefits we can realize. We become more realistic, intuitive, creative, independent, flexible, generous, respectful, fair, cooperative, able to manage change, and willing to accept our mistakes and correct them, and if that isn't enough to fight for authenticity, I don't know what is! Living authentically earns the trust of others because people feel safe and comfortable in the presence of honesty and realness.

Bottom line; authenticity is attractive. It has an aura about it, and people can feel it. When you're being real, it's palpable, and people admire it. And when we're being inauthentic, that is sensed too, and it is less appealing to others. So, in actuality, authenticity is the manifestation of honesty, and you would think that's how we want to be, and present ourselves always. But, unfortunately for us we don't because we fall into the trap of believing we have to be something other than who we are to be admired or liked more. Sometimes it's just not enough to enjoy those benefits I enumerated when we walk the authentic path. We feel we have to do more, or be more than we are, and that can be a self-imposed expectation we've placed on ourselves, or have allowed someone else to place on us.

The *authentic self* is not who we think we should be, or supposed to be based on someone else's idea or expectation, even if that person is the eighth doctor in your family lineage, and ready to pass their stethoscope onto you. The authentic self is the "real deal", the "genuine substance", the "real McCoy" and anything other than that is false and untrue. If you've been inauthentic to yourself, it's probably made you unhappy, and you may not even know why, and it might take a very long time to wake up to the reality that you're living a life that doesn't feel honest, and you don't know how that happened.

*Mindfulness helps us not forget who we are. It keeps us present and aware, and if, or when we might feel an impulse to be inauthentic, it reminds us immediately that falseness of any kind feels wrong with every fiber of our being.*

When we're mindful, we have heightened awareness, and with heightened awareness it's hard to be dishonest with ourselves. It's like having an inner lie detector, or truth barometer that goes off inside us, and makes it almost impossible not to pay attention to it. Even if someone is suggesting what we should do, or who we should be, we get a signal loud and clear that no one can decide who we are, and only we can determine our authenticity.

Basically, Mindfulness doesn't let you escape yourself, unless you choose to hide who you really are, and if so, being present with honesty is something you will avoid. If that's what you find yourself doing, ask what you have to gain from that. Why keep trying to avoid or escape the real you? Isn't that taxing or exhausting? It takes a lot of energy to keep up a false image of yourself, which is like always having a mask or a disguise on, but once you surrender to your most authentic self, you can feel so much lighter, and most likely relieved to let the burdens of deception go.

Mindfulness will always keep you connected to, and on top of what is going on with you, and everything around you. And when you're present, you're more connected to your truth, and when you're connected to your truth, you live honestly.

It works seamlessly with your true nature because you're functioning as you are meant to; honestly, naturally, and in the complete flow of who you really are.

When you're present in the moment with total awareness, you become finely tuned to anything that feels out of step or not in alignment with who you are. And when we step out of Mindfulness, we can immediately feel that we are not fully aware, or connected to ourselves completely. It's like having brain fog. The goal is to live each moment by being present, so that when you start to feel fuzzy, or not quite right, you catch it immediately and know that you have stepped out of the "Mindfulness zone" and are about to compromise your most authentic self.

But let's say you're completely present in a moment, and find yourself feeling some discomfort about how blatantly honest you're being about yourself. Sometimes being honest can be very difficult or painful, and depending on what you tell yourself, even brutal. On the path of self-realization, it's necessary to stay honest, but it's extremely important to choose what you say carefully.

When you practice Mindfulness, you are not a harsh critic, but instead a *constructive advisor*.

That means you're guiding or counseling yourself productively, and what you're telling yourself is useful and constructive. Honesty, when used aggressively, or meanly towards oneself, is not honesty, but unkindness, or even cruelty. Don't mistake one for the other. Honesty is not meant to hurt, but to help. And if what you're telling yourself isn't helping you, then stop telling yourself whatever it is that's making you feel bad or horrible about yourself, and start supporting your authentic self with advice that can truly help you strive to be your most conscious self. This means telling yourself only things that support you being the best version of your authentic self. Even if you're putting your focus and awareness on areas you would genuinely like to change or improve, then do it consciously.

For example, we don't realize how much of our inner talk begins with, "I'm not" or "I can't" or "I'll never" or saying things affirmatively like, "I'm not good at" or "I'm incapable" or "I'm not qualified" or "I'm inadequate". The authentic self knows exactly what its strengths and weaknesses are, but it doesn't define itself as inadequate, or unqualified, or anything that boxes itself into limited beliefs. The authentic self is kind and forgiving, and knows that by being committed to honesty, it sharpens and strengthens its authenticity even more.

Your realness can only get more real. And when you allow that to happen, you can experience a power that is way beyond anything that keeps falseness, or dishonesty alive in you.

Dishonesty is for those that can't handle the truth of who they really are. I want you to know that your real, "raw to the core" self is what's most beautiful about you. That's right. Your realness is beautiful, and your falseness is not. The very thing that you're hiding about yourself, and afraid of showing to someone, can be the very thing that someone will love the most about you. You may not feel that way, and might be rolling your eyes and thinking, "Yeah, right!" But when you decide to show off who you really are, and expose your truth in all of its "everything", and that means imperfections, which we all have, you'll no longer need to hide your human blemishes, but instead embrace them as part of your "perfection."

Vladimir Horowitz, the famous pianist and composer, once said, "Perfection itself is imperfection." May we let our imperfections be seen, and celebrate all of who we are, and I mean entirely. And when we can be fully honest with ourselves, we can then be honest with others. But we must practice the same act of Mindfulness we do with ourselves when telling those around us what we think.

Honesty will always be a choice we have, be it with ourselves, or with others, and at every given moment, we can choose the higher road of honesty, and say what is truthful, or we can withhold it, and keep it to ourselves. Again, it's a choice we can make, and sometimes we make it because we're afraid to speak the truth, or maybe it's because we want to protect someone from knowing something we think might hurt them. Each of us will come upon a time when we're afraid to speak the truth, and either face our fear honestly, or deny it to ourselves.

We will also face whether it's better to tell someone the truth, or conceal it from them because we feel, "What they don't know cannot hurt them."

"Honesty," Benjamin Franklin said, "is the best policy." If you strongly feel that withholding a piece of information from someone is the better thing to do, then maybe you will consider your choice not an act of dishonesty, but an act of kindness. Whatever you choose to do, whether to reveal the truth or conceal it, do it from an honest place within yourself, and let that guide you. But don't let fear be your reason not to speak the truth because that will always do more harm than good, and can hurt someone even more by withholding what they need to know.

But where honesty will always be most challenging is being honest with ourselves, which is why we must work on it the hardest.

We may think we're being honest with ourselves, but the way to know for certain is if we let Mindfulness lead the way, so that we have a much stronger chance of staying on the honesty track. Stay present, be real, and check in with your authentic barometer daily. Take what I've called your "spiritual pulse", so you can know exactly what is churning inside your heart, and why. That will keep you honest. Ask yourself questions like, "Am I being honest?" or "Am I being real?" or "Am I being authentic?" Aspire to be honest, real, and authentic, and you'll stand a greater chance of being all of those things consistently.

But, we also know that there are some people, who out of fear or insecurity, are so dishonest, that it can border on deception or delusion. Who's going to set them straight if what they think or believe about themselves has them so convinced they're right, that any attempt to be honest can be met with them thinking you're the one who's lying or being dishonest. But as Lao Tzu observes in his quote above, "Be also honest to those who are not honest. Thus honesty is attained."

But pick and choose carefully who you're being honest with. If you sense that someone is resistant, or unable to hear what you have to say, even if you're intention or motive is to help them, it's better not to speak your truth because you run the risk of inciting anger in them, which then will be projected onto you.

We also need to be aware of how honesty can be misleading. We may think we're being honest about something, but actually dishonest in our intention without consciously knowing it. We may not mean to mislead someone, but out of our own fear or insecurity, we can say something for reasons that are not straightforward because we have some type of agenda to get what we want, or do it because we need to make ourselves feel better.

For example, you can tell someone not to take a job because it requires travelling, but it really may be because you don't want that person to be away from you, even though it could be a good job. Or you tell a friend you don't think they should be with the person they're involved with romantically because you find them unappealing or threatening in some way, which might be because you're jealous, or unhappy that they're spending so much time with them, and it's taking their time away from you. Be clear in your honesty, and check to see if you're doing it for your own personal gain, or to truly help someone, and considering first what might be best for them.

> ***Honesty, when combined with Mindfulness,***
> ***is having a keen awareness of what it is***
> ***we want to convey, and why.***

When we communicate from a mindful place, we are so clear about what it is we want to say, and the reasons for why we want to say it that there's no doubt in our minds about our intentions. It's as if Mindfulness holds us accountable for being both truthful and honest in such a way that it feels almost impossible to say anything to someone unless there is absolutely no uncertainty about our motive behind it. And even if what needs to be conveyed to someone is difficult, challenging, or even hurtful because it's a sensitive subject or issue, it will be heard gently because of the thoughtful or caring way in which it was said.

Each day we have some type of honesty test that we face. It could be choosing not to be honest with ourselves because we just might not be in the mood to take a hard or closer look at ourselves, or not being honest with loved ones or friends, which can come up in a myriad of ways. It might be when our partner or friend asks us to do something that we don't really want to do, and we come up with an excuse, or telling our partner or friend what they want to hear because it strokes their ego, but we don't agree with the choice they might be making for themselves, or it could be even more serious than that. It can be not being honest about how we feel in our relationship or marriage. We may be afraid to tell our partner what we really feel, or need, in the event that they won't give it to us, or be angry for us asking. Or it could be that we don't love them in the same way we once did, so we tell them something that is dishonest instead, and before you know it you're living dishonestly, and end up hurting your partner even more because you weren't honest with them from the beginning. It could be not being honest with your children, and telling them only nice and loving things because you feel you have to protect them. That can mean boosting them up to feed their confidence or self esteem, and yet what might be better for them is to be direct and honest, which you can do nicely and lovingly, but tell them they aren't always going to win, or be picked, or excel, or even liked.

Honesty is a practice, and we can become better at it the more we do it. Like Sigmund Freud said, "Being entirely honest with oneself is a good exercise." When we speak the truth from our higher self, we find ourselves speaking words that matter and have value, and that is when our honesty is combined with integrity, and how we aspire to live our lives daily.

When we're honest mindfully, and choosing to communicate on a more conscious level, we are contributing to a higher good, as was discussed in Chapter 13 (Desire). We know that speaking honestly will benefit others, and we are motivated to do it whenever possible, and as mindfully as we can.

So, what drives your honesty? Is it the need to clear your conscience? Is it a genuine desire to speak the truth, or to help others by telling them something you think will be beneficial for them? Does it make you feel good to be honest, or does it make you uncomfortable? Does it make you feel more authentic? How would you feel if you couldn't be honest?

Can you think of a time you were honest, and someone thanked you from the bottom of their heart? Or a time you spoke honestly, and it disappointed someone, or was hurtful, and it made you doubt your honesty. Being honest isn't always easy to do, and it can make you feel awful when it's caused someone pain or suffering, or it can make you feel like the bad guy when you had to be the one to expose something, and call someone out that did something wrong.

Being honest is a big responsibility, and how we handle it either makes us feel good about ourselves, or makes us doubt if we're capable of doing it well.

Bottom line: honesty is something we are either comfortable with or not, and if you're not, ask yourself what is it about honesty that makes you uncomfortable. It's okay if you've hurt somebody by being honest, if not hurting anyone was your intention. It's the knowing that you had to be honest, or else you would feel dishonest, and you couldn't live with it that matters. And it's also okay to be the "bad guy" by being honest.

Not everyone is going to like you if you speak the truth. They may even resent you for it, and turn against you. There's a reason for the phrase, "Kill the messenger." But again, you have to weigh that with what is more important to you. To either speak the truth because you know you have to, and it's for a higher good, or go along with the lie to keep things as they are, can be more damaging than good.

Each of us has to look honesty in the face and ask ourselves who we are with it. We have to decide if we're someone that will choose to be honest no matter what, or be able to forgive ourselves when we felt we couldn't be honest. But ask yourself why you can't if that's the choice you make. Are you afraid to be honest, and if so, why? Are you embarrassed, and if so, what's awkward about it for you? Do you feel it's not your right to speak up and be honest, and if so, who has more of a right than you do to be heard? Do you prefer avoiding confrontations, and being honest feels confrontational, or you just don't like rocking the boat? Whatever makes you uncomfortable around being honest, find out by digging a little deeper within your heart and soul. No one is judging you, but yourself.

Honesty is not meant to hurt or punish ourselves or someone else, but to teach us how to be a better and more genuine person, and call upon our higher self when we are faced with a decision to choose honesty over anything else. But maybe in our honesty we decide to do nothing, or be silent. Sometimes in our silence we are being honest, but we must know if our silence is being passive, or if our silence is a choice to not participate in anger, or hate, or violence. That can be honesty too.

Honesty doesn't always have words. It can be when we know it's time to put down our weapons, or walk away from something that we know must end. Raising a white flag can be considered an act of honesty. It says peace over war, and when we're resigned to stop hurting or killing one another, honesty can speak so loudly that there is nothing more to say.

Auden wrote, "We must love one another or die." There is nothing more honest than that.

But above all, be honest with yourself. Your honesty is what you have to live with. Even if you take a step back from it out of fear or insecurity, or for whatever reasons, know that you can step right back into the flow of your deepest "authentic truth" which is the greatest honesty to realize about yourself.

# Meditation for Honesty

1. Sit somewhere quiet.

2. Close your eyes.

3. Be aware of any sounds, thoughts, feelings or sensations in your body. Simply observe them.

4. Take a few deep breaths in and out.

5. Say silently, "I choose honesty."

6. Say silently, "I choose honesty consciously."

7. Say silently, "I choose honesty with compassion."

8. Say silently, "Let me be honest with myself."

9. When you are ready, bring your focus and awareness back to your body.

10. Slowly open your eyes.

11. *When you are ready, transition out of your meditation.*

*Note to self:*

*I am present with my honesty*
*I choose honesty over dishonesty*
*Let me be wise and courageous in my honesty*

# CHAPTER 21

# **Authenticity**

*But above all, in order to be, never try to seem.*
*—Albert Camus*

*This above all:*
*To thine own self be true,*
*And it must follow, as the night the day,*
*Thou canst not then be false to any man.*
*—Shakespeare*

Who are you really, if not who you really are? That may sound like some kind of Zen koan, which is a paradox, or a puzzle for Zen Buddhist monks to meditate on to gain enlightenment. Perhaps we won't reach enlightenment by contemplating that question, but we can certainly find out who we are, by knowing who we're not.

If we ask ourselves, "Who am I?" we will automatically answer with our name, or what it is we do for a living, our role, or our persona, such as "I'm a mother", "I'm a doctor", "I'm an actor", "I'm a carpenter" or even; "I'm an addict". We may be any one of those things, or a combination of them. But unless we know who we are other than just our "identity" or what we do, we might not know if we're being true to ourselves, or authentic in whatever identity we've taken on.

Maybe somewhere in your role as a mother, you're conflicted about having given up a career to be a parent, or maybe torn about working, and leaving your children at home or daycare. Or, maybe if you were/are an addict, you were once on top of the world, but lost confidence in yourself at one point in your life, and couldn't handle failure so you numbed yourself with drugs or alcohol. Or maybe you became a doctor because it was expected of you to be one since you come from generations of physicians, as I spoke about in the previous chapter on honesty.

Who we are might not be what we wanted, or intended to be at all, but we've been that person for so long, who would we be otherwise? Some people just fall into being who they are, or inherit being who they are, or are told to be who they are. Others knew who they wanted to be when they spoke their first words. But whether you announced your identity at your first dance recital, or you smiled compliantly when your father announced at your Bar Mitzvah that you were going to be a lawyer just like him, somewhere on the "Who am I?" train, you woke up and realized that you got on the wrong one, became inauthentic to yourself, and don't know how that happened.

There's a great song by The Talking Heads, called "Once in a Lifetime," that really sums it up:

*And you may find yourself*
*Living in a shotgun shack*
*And you may find yourself*
*In another part of the world*
*And you may find yourself*
*Behind the wheel of a large automobile*
*And you may find yourself in a beautiful house*
*With a beautiful wife*
*And you may ask yourself, well*
*How did I get here?*

It's very conceivable that you can wake up one day and ask yourself, "How did I get here?" A good way to avoid that from happening is to ask yourself, "Who am I?" long before you end up somewhere you really don't want to be, or flummoxed by how the hell you let yourself get there.

**Mindfulness helps us not forget who we are.**
**It keeps us present and aware, and if, or when we might**
**feel an impulse to be inauthentic, it reminds us**
**immediately that falseness of any kind feels wrong**
**with every fiber of our being.**

When we're mindful, we have heightened awareness, and with heightened awareness it's hard to be dishonest with ourselves. It's like having an inner lie detector, as I've spoken of, or truth barometer that goes off inside us, and makes it almost impossible not to pay attention to it. Even if someone is suggesting what we should do, or who we should be, as I mentioned, we get a signal loud and clear that no one can decide who we are, and only we can determine our authenticity.

But whether you decided who your authentic self was long ago, somewhere on the life path you can either forget it, doubt it, turn away from it, give it away, or even make a decision that you dislike or hate who you really are, and deny ever being that person. It's like an identity swap, only instead of taking on a role that isn't you because you felt you had to, you gave your authentic self away gladly, and after living so long as someone you're not, you're now desperately looking for who you are, like a mother trying to find the baby she gave up for adoption. The good news is you can always find that person you once were, and when you become reunited with your authentic self, it can be the greatest, and most freeing day of your life.

It's not easy living a life trapped in inauthenticity, and it takes work to pretend to be someone we're not. It can also be very painful to be seen, liked, or even loved for a false self, and terrifying that if, or when you're found out that you've lived dishonestly, not only can you be met with tremendous anger and resentment, but be blamed or accused for harming others in some type of way, be it emotionally or psychologically.

An example of that is when somebody comes out as gay, or transgender, and their partner or family has deep resentment towards them for what they perceive as an act of horrible dishonesty or unthinkable deception. Nobody sets out to hurt others in their inauthenticity to themselves. They are struggling to find their truth, and sometimes it takes them feeling comfortable or safe enough to reveal what they have been hiding, or perhaps lying to themselves about for a very long time. We must have compassion for those that have been unable to be authentic, and know that they never meant to hurt anyone more than they've hurt themselves in the denial of their authentic self.

Being authentic is natural. Being inauthentic is not, and yet, time and time again we can slip into not being true about something, whether it's about the choices we make in our life, or the role we've taken on, and now consider it our identity.

This "human experience" I've talked about can be challenging, to say the least, and sometimes we feel that we have to be something we're not to stay in a relationship, or be accepted, or not ostracized from our family. But it will always be our higher self, our "spiritual being" that knows the truth of who we are, and if we don't let it come forward, we will suffer again and again in whatever dishonest "human experience" we are having, and resign ourselves to living a life of inauthenticity.

In America, we've got a lot of freedom to be who we are, so you wonder why would we mess with that freedom. It's not like we have to be something or someone that we're not, and even if the pressure to be someone other than who we really are happened to us early on in our life, we can lift that pressure off of ourselves by deciding to let our authentic self be seen.

Most pressure is self-imposed, but it's easy to blame others for feeling that we're trapped in something. You've got the key. Open up the cage you've placed yourself in, and fly out.

Even if a parent told you you'll never amount to anything, so you stopped trying to excel at something, or a teacher said that you weren't good at writing, so you decided you'll never be an author, or a friend insinuated that you were unattractive, so you never felt worthy to find a partner and get married, you still have a choice to reclaim your authentic self, and can do it at any time. And that means one day you find yourself the CEO of a company, or writing a book, or walking down the aisle with the person of your dreams.

That's because you reclaimed your authentic self, and no matter what anybody told you, you knew it wasn't true, and it was just a matter of time before you were going to prove them wrong.

But there are people in other countries who unfortunately do not have the choices or freedom to live their authentic self. As we know, certain countries which practice fundamentalism will actually harm or kill you if you step out of the identity, role, persona, or whatever is imposed on you, which could affect what you wear, or how you think and communicate. That is a tragedy.

What tremendous freedom there is in authenticity! Who wouldn't want to appreciate or celebrate being true, and real, and genuine? It's so liberating to be who we really are, unless you yourself are torn about your authentic self, and not allowing yourself to live it out.

You might feel ashamed to admit who you are, or conflicted, or afraid. Maybe you're not sure about your sexual identity, or if you are sure, you may be afraid to show or reveal it because you feel you'll be judged or rejected. Or maybe you're uncertain about your political leanings, but feel you have to go along with your friends, or your community. Or maybe you come from a conservative family with strong religious beliefs, and you don't want to adopt those beliefs as yours, but if you don't, you'll be cut off from members of your family. Or maybe it's looking or dressing a certain way to be accepted by others, or have your partner find you desirable. There are so many reasons we choose inauthenticity over authenticity, which is why being present in your life this very moment can change all of that.

Mindfulness let's us see ourselves for who we really are in the "here and now", and when we're fully present and aware of how we feel about ourselves right now, in the present, we know that we must act on it because we have to.

We are so connected to what we are feeling in the moment, that even if it's a feeling of uncertainty, we are prepared to go deeper within ourselves for the right answers.

**_Mindfulness gives us the opportunity to lift the veils of the inauthentic self, by being aware of how oppressive those veils are._**

We feel everything when we are fully awake and aware in a moment, and just like it feels uncomfortable to have a piece of clothing on that's itchy or irritating to our skin, we know we need to remove it, and that will solve the problem. Mindfulness helps you be a good problem solver because it focuses your attention on the very thing that needs to be addressed or fixed.

We know not to waste a single moment when we are mindful, and that means that being inauthentic in any way is not only wasteful of that moment, but robs us off living that moment as real as it possibly can be, which we choose not to do because the moments of our lives are so important and valuable to us that we want to savor them, and experience them as beautifully and authentically as we can.

And that's what authenticity is: ***it's a choice to be real***. We have that choice every moment of our lives. We can choose to be real and authentic, or we can choose to be inauthentic and to live a lie. But when you are committed to the truth, and choose honesty as a way to express it, it's very difficult to give into inauthenticity of any kind. By staying on the path of Mindfulness, it will keep your moments more honest and "seamless". You will live your life in the way of harmony, which is being true to your nature, and ultimately true to your most authentic self.

# Meditation for Authenticity

1. Sit somewhere quiet.

2. Close your eyes.

3. Be aware of any sounds, feelings, thoughts or sensations you may be feeling in your body. Simply observe them.

4. Put your focus and awareness onto your breath.

5. Take a few deep breaths in and out.

6. Say silently, "I am authentic."

7. Say silently, "I live my life authentically."

8. Say silently, "There is no other way to live than being authentic."

9. When you are ready, bring your focus and attention back to your body.

10. Slowly open your eyes.

11. *When you are ready transition out of your meditation.*

*Note to self:*

*I am authentic*
*I live in harmony with who I am*
*I am true to my nature*

CHAPTER 22

# Compassion

*Love and compassion are necessities, not luxuries.*
*Without them humanity cannot survive.*
*—Dalai Lama*

In Buddhism, a Bodhisattva is an "ordinary person" who devotes their life to the way of a Buddha, which means they practice compassion as the Buddha did. They don't need to wear a saffron robe, or live on a mountaintop with monks, but if they live their life caring about the wellness of all living beings, they are walking the path of the Bodhisattva, someone who is motivated by great compassion.

Each one of us can be motivated by compassion, and can do our part in caring for others in a variety of ways. As I mentioned in Chapter 16 (Behavior), "When you practice Mindfulness, you are present and more aware. You see when someone is indicating that they would like to go in front of you in traffic, or when you're walking in front of another person, you hold the door open for them, instead of letting it swing shut in their face."

Mindfulness reminds you that even the smallest gestures shows a genuine caring for our fellow man, and if every person on the planet did one thing daily to help someone in need, we would live in a world that makes compassion a priority, and what a wonderful world that would be.

Mindfulness will always keep you on the compassion track. When you're present, and your awareness is heightened, you can't but be aware of others.

But if you're walking around in a me-centric bubble, there is so much you miss. Even if you walked right past someone who was down and out, you could easily ignore them, and not really care what condition they might be in, or feel it's your job to do anything to help. And now with so many people walking around with their faces glued to their cell phones, we're becoming more oblivious, and the type of human contact we're having with one another is becoming even more impersonal, and less compassionate.

If we are committed to the path of spiritual awakening, and a shift in our consciousness, we know that our own awakening is to the benefit of others awakening, and we view our spiritual growth as something that can not only help us on our life journey, but also help others on theirs.

Compassion becomes an integral part of our spiritual work, and we are truly motivated by it to help awaken everyone we come into contact with, in hopes that they can see the light and love in their hearts, and be inspired to do the same for others. Together we can help spread less suffering on the planet, and carry on a goal for universal awakening. This is the chain; the collective that each of us are a part of, and again, it's a reminder that "What you do with your today, and what I do with my today, effects all of the todays of everyone on the planet."

But compassion must always begin towards ourselves first. In our awareness through practicing Mindfulness, we know that the love and caring we show for ourselves, exemplifies how it's done, and this is what others see. If we cannot love and care for ourselves, we certainly cannot do the same for anyone else. And this includes the thoughts that we tell ourselves, which although may be hidden from others to see, we know what they are, and must take responsibility for having them.

When you are motivated by compassion, your thoughts support the caring you have for yourself and others. But there will be times when we will step out of the moment, and get caught up in life's challenges, and our thoughts of compassion are not what will be occupying our mind. Again, I have to say that it will be our human experiences that will always pull us away from our "spiritual being"—and yes, we're human, and must recognize that although we may aspire to walk the path of Buddha, we will be tested time and time again of our commitment to not put ourselves first before others.

It's clear, as I said in Chapter 13 (Desire), that we have desires, and they are normal to have. But when we seek to satisfy only our own needs, we can lose sight of wanting to satisfy a greater desire that can benefit the goodness of all. When we begin each day wanting love and kindness for everyone, ourselves included, that is when we move through life in the highest state of Mindfulness because our awareness of others is how we see constantly, and what we hold in our perception is large enough to contain the whole world, and that is when we are living true compassion.

This, of course, is not always an easy task to do, which is why committing to our practices, be it meditation, yoga, or whatever we do that takes us more out of our "human experience" and lets our "spiritual being" come forward is so important to do. The ultimate goal is to have our "spiritual being" present with us always, which it is, but when we get bogged down in the doing, we overshadow it with our more basic needs. You know what that's like when you're rushing around doing what you need to do. You may find yourself at the bank, and the line is long, and guess who's not present in that line with you, your higher self; your "spiritual being." That's right, it seems nowhere in sight when your inner dialogue is telling you to hurry up, and get to where you have to go next. Or how about when someone cuts you off in traffic. Forget about being in a thoughtful state of mind to let someone go in front of you. This is a moment when someone unexpectedly dumps their human experience onto you, and you're left with completely forgetting about your "spiritual being" and wanting to either swear at them, or maybe even go after them.

As humans, we have so much to learn all the time. Having compassion is, by far, our greatest teacher.

So how would you rate your compassion? Don't feel bad if you rate it low. The truth is it's not that you aren't a compassionate person, which I'm sure you are, it's that our lives get so busy with everything we think we have to do to make us happier, we just forget to stop, and think globally. I mean, it's difficult to always be thinking globally when you're busy trying to go after your own personal goals (unless your goal is to help stop world hunger). Or maybe your goal is to help women in Darfur who have to walk miles and miles to get water for their family, and have donated a water-well nearby. Or maybe you feed the homeless every Thanksgiving, or help build homes in impoverished countries, or are the first to jump on a plane when a population of people like the Native American Indians in North Dakota are having their land stolen out from under them, yet again, and a pipeline being built under it will not only effect them, but all of us. Or, conversely, you may think that the Missouri River that the pipeline runs through isn't your river, so why should you be concerned about it? But if we think compassionately, and globally, then all of the rivers are our rivers, and all of the people are our people. This is why when those tragic events happened in France, one of the hashtags that immediately went viral was "Je Suis Charlie." In solidarity and compassion, we all became Charlie Hebdo when the staff of that magazine was slaughtered so mercilessly. If I'm not Charlie Hebdo, and you're not Charlie Hebdo, then who are we really? This harkens back to the quote by rabbinic sage Hillel the Elder, "If I am not for myself, who will be for me? If I am only for myself, what am I? If not now, when?"

As the Dalai Lama said in the quote above, "Love and compassion are necessities, not luxuries...(and) without them humanity cannot survive." This is why we must commit ourselves to compassion, because if we don't, then we are committing to the possibility that we may not be able to survive.

One simple act of compassion supports our humanity, and we don't have to go so far out of our way to do it.

Think of how you can leave your house today, and what it is you want to take out into your world. Your world, in your city, in your life, in your mini universe, represents the entire world, and so is the same with everyone in their own mini universes. We are the micro/macrocosm, and we can make a difference in both. Think big, and act bigger. Or, as Gandhi said, "Be the change you want to see in the world."

Begin with one act of compassion. Think globally by acting locally from your heart.

# Meditation for Compassion

1. Sit somewhere quiet.

2. Close your eyes gently.

3. Be aware of any sounds, thoughts, feelings or sensations in your body. Simply observe them.

4. Put your focus and awareness onto your breath.

5. Take a few deep breaths in and out.

6. Say silently, "I feel compassion for myself and others."

7. Say silently, "May all beings realize love and peace."

8. Repeat this as many times as you wish.

9. When you're ready, bring your focus and awareness back to your body.

10. Slowly open your eyes.

11. *When you are ready, transition out of your meditation.*

### Note to self:

*I choose to live my life compassionately*
*Compassion is in my heart always*
*I feel compassion for all*

# CHAPTER 23

# Purpose

*Do what you love. Know your own bone; gnaw at it,*
*bury it, unearth it, and gnaw it still.*
—Henry David Thoreau

*The mystery of human existence lies not in just staying*
*alive, but in finding something to live for.*
—Fyodor Dostoyevsky

Each of us has a purpose. We may think it's the very thing that we're doing, but it's how we're doing it that can make the biggest difference in what our purpose is, and what it means to us. Purpose is having a reason to do something, and that doesn't mean that your reason has to be that you want to do something important or great in your life; like help stop world hunger, but whatever it is that you do, do it well, and that becomes your reason for doing it.

Some people do things without really caring about how they're doing it. As a matter of fact, they don't even like what they're doing, and it shows.

Have you ever gone into a store, and the salesperson acts like they're doing you a favor by saying "hello"? Or maybe you've had a waiter that acts like they'd rather be doing anything than taking your order. Or maybe it's a tele-marketer, and they sound like you're the reason for their misery. We've all encountered people that aren't happy doing what they're doing. When that happens, it makes us feel like we're a reminder of how much they really don't like their job, and it doesn't always feel so good to be the recipient of their unhappiness.

Sometimes it's hard not to take it personally. But wouldn't it be great if we could, in a nice, loving way, say to that person, "I get it, you're not happy doing your job, but what would make you happier? Tell me, I'm here to listen." It might make them think about it, hug you, and put in their resignation, or give their two weeks notice right then or there. Or you run the risk of them being insulted and wanting to bite your head off. But that very question, "What would make you happier?" deserves to be asked. It is the very thing that could make someone wake up to the fact that, yes, they're truly unhappy doing what they're doing, and now's the time to do something about it.

When we're not happy doing what we're doing, we can feel purposeless or empty, but we might not know what to do about it so we just accept feeling that way, and continue doing the thing that's making us feel purposeless or empty.

Millions of people are resigned to the fact that they're going to be doing the same thing, day in and day out, for the rest of their lives, and being unhappy is just the way it is.

No, being unhappy isn't just the way it is, but we tell ourselves it is, and when we tell ourselves things like that, it becomes our reality.

It's astonishing what people accept for themselves. That they're willing to just lay down for something that doesn't call to their heart and soul, and let that thing walk all over them, and remind them again and again how empty they feel inside. But when you wake up and realize that this is your life, and it's short, that's when you know you've got to take that unhappiness by the throat and tell it who's boss.

That doesn't mean that you have to quit your job tomorrow, which you could if you felt strongly that it's the thing to do, but when we begin to ask ourselves questions like "Who am I?" or "What would make me happy?" we can find out things we might not have given ourselves a chance to know.

So many people live their lives never asking themselves how they're doing, or if they're happy or not, because they don't feel they should, or have a right to. But that spiritual pulse I suggested you take of yourself is the very thing you need to do to find out what's really going on with you, and whether you're happy or not, and yes, you should do it, and yes, you have every right to do it.

Here's what can help you start things off:

Make a date with yourself. Take yourself somewhere nice, like a walk on the beach or garden path, and ask yourself how you're doing. I bet that just you walking on the beach or in the garden will already feel so good for you, that you'll wonder why you didn't do it sooner.

One of the reasons we're so unhappy is that we live our lives completely out of balance. Many people work to live— they don't have a choice but to keep on working to pay the rent or feed their babies—and some people live to work because they're workaholics. But whichever is your reason, check your spiritual pulse, and find out what you need to do to connect to your buried "happy place." We've all got one, and maybe you're so out of touch with yours, you're convinced that's something you can only get at McDonalds.

No, your happy place is there, inside the depth of your being. But if you don't practice Mindfulness, and take time to go within to find out who your authentic self is, which is more than what you do, or your identity, then you're going to continue living your life going from moment to moment doing what you think you have to do, or supposed to do, or expected to do; not as your most real self, and feel unhappy while you're doing it.

Even if you have to do a job that you think is menial, that doesn't mean you have to be miserable doing it. Whatever your job is, if you feel you have to do it for whatever reasons, then find time in your day or week to do something else that makes you feel good, like walking on the beach, or planting a garden, or feeding the homeless, which will connect you to your compassion, and always make you feel grateful for just being alive, and able to put food in your own mouth.

Our happiness is relative, and if we feel that our glass is half empty, and can't fill it up ourselves because we're waiting for it to magically fill up on its own, as I referenced in Chapter 2 (This Magic Moment), then we're always going to look at our glass that way, and think that we're being "robbed of those magical moments".

Each moment of our lives is magical, as I said, and even if you're truly miserable in your job, or doing whatever it is that keeps making you feel miserable, you need to stop, breathe, and tell yourself how lucky you are to be alive. Once you do that, you can get down to business to find out what you need to do next to support your authentic self. If you don't connect to your true self, then nothing you do will have the essence or thumbprint of you on it, and, of course, you will feel empty.

Conversely, there are those people that absolutely love what they do, and that's because they put their heart into what it is and you feel it, or sense it, or taste it. How about those people that love to cook or bake, and they put so much good energy into the meal they made you, or those cupcakes they brought over to your house, that you not only taste the deliciousness of them, but there's something else added, and that ingredient is their love, and that's what you're tasting more than anything.

I've had waiters that put a big smile on my face, or even said something profound to me worthy of a quote right up there with Buddha, or Gandhi, or Martin Luther King Jr., and that's because their heart is into what they're doing, and you feel it, and that's what makes them great. *Greatness isn't measured by what you do, but by how well you do it.*

When you bring your authentic self to whatever you do, and you do it really, really well, you truly can rock it like any famous rock star. Who you are can make a difference in someone's life by how you are being, and how you feel about what you're doing.

Remember your "spiritual being" is having a "human experience", so let your higher self shine whenever you can, whether you're waiting tables, selling clothes, soliciting something over the phone, or whatever it is you do.

You might even be someone who has the job of the century, one that could be the envy of anyone who knows you, but if your heart isn't into it, or you live your life out of balance, it won't satisfy you, and you'll be pining for something else—that "happy place" you feel is out of reach for you. But it's there, deep within, and you'll find it if you look for it.

So, you have a choice, either do what you do well, or decide to do something else, if what you're doing genuinely makes you unhappy. Make a game plan for yourself, and in the process find your purpose even if it's searching for your purpose. That means find the reason for what you're looking for, and there's no greater reason than advocating for yourself to be your most authentic self, and putting that into something that genuinely moves your heart.

# Meditation for Purpose

1. Sit somewhere quiet.

2. Close your eyes.

3. Be aware of any sounds, thoughts, feelings or sensations in your body. Simply observe them.

4. Put your focus and awareness onto your breath.

5. Take a few deep breaths in and out.

6. Say silently, "What is my purpose?"

7. Say silently, "Am I living my purpose?

8. Say silently, "I am ready to live my purpose."

9. When you're ready, bring your focus and awareness back to your body.

10. Slowly open your eyes.

11. *When you are ready, transition out of your meditation.*

*Note to self:*

*I am connected to my purpose*
*I am proud of my purpose*
*I enjoy sharing my purpose with others*

# CHAPTER 24

# Intention

*Our intention creates our reality.*
*—Wayne Dyer*

Think of intention as the mojo behind your purpose, which is like sprinkling some magic on what you want to do, and then making it happen. Since you've already got the magic, there's no telling what you can do, and what you can create.

Remember, magic isn't something outside of you. It's something you possess, and by manifesting whatever you want, it can seem magical when it actually comes to fruition.

You know when you've worked hard at something, and the results are pretty great? It could be something you've made, like a piece of art, or you've written a book. Or maybe it's something you designed, like a house, or a line of clothing. Or maybe you planted a vegetable garden, or put together something really big, like a retreat, or a festival, and you almost can't believe you pulled it off.

That shows how powerful you are in your intentions, and yes, you've got the magic in you to do it. But it wasn't magic alone that made it happen.

You had to be fully present in your intention, because if you weren't, your intention wouldn't have been clear and precise, and magic couldn't have met it. As I said in Chapter 2 (This Magic Moment), "Magic doesn't want to chase you. Magic doesn't want to work that hard. Magic wants you to be ready and receptive to it." When you are ready and receptive, and your intentions are set, watch out world for what is possible!

You see, when we're present, and fully focused on the moment we are in, that's when we can zero in on our intention in such a way that it's laser sharp. There's no telling what amazing things we are capable of creating when our focus and awareness are that clear.

But while we must ask ourselves questions like, "Who am I?" and; "What is my purpose?" we must then follow them with, "What is my intention?" Questions like these hold us accountable for not only who we are, but what it is we want to do in our life, and how we plan on doing it *consciously.*

Having an intention is how we should begin each day, and each day our intention can be something different.

We may decide that our intention is to change our life, which is a bold and daring intention to have, and by deciding what steps we will take for that to happen, we can take that first move in that direction. *Many people say they want to change their lives, but it's the ones that carry through on their intentions that actually do.*

When you check in with yourself daily, and take your spiritual pulse, you will be ready to know what your intention is for that day. Mindfulness reminds us to be present so that we can be in the moment with total awareness to check in with ourselves. When we stop what we're doing, and devote some time to connect to our higher self, our "spiritual being", that is when we can hear the voice of our intention loud and clear, and once we do, we are ready to act on it.

In our awareness, we are more conscious, and when we are more conscious, we are more expansive. What we can hold in our expansiveness can be intentions that are not just for our own personal gain, but also for the joy and benefit of others. The beauty of having intentions that are inclusive of others is that we get to enjoy what makes other people happy, and that can be extremely gratifying.

Some people hold such large, benevolent intentions that they create things that affect thousands, even millions of people. People like Bill and Melinda Gates, who created a foundation that support programs and positive change across the globe like agricultural development, global health, emergency relief, and education. Talk about huge intentions! And then there's someone like Malala Yousafzai, the Pakistani activist who was shot because her intention was to defend her right—and all women's right—to an education. Her intention got her the Nobel Peace Prize, which just goes to show you that there is no intention, big or small, that can't create something profound and special. If it's from a place in your heart that's well intended, you can affect not only your life, but also the lives of others in the most extraordinary way.

As I said in Chapter 22 (Compassion), "Think globally by acting locally from your heart." Set an intention daily, and let it be from a place within yourself that is motivated by compassion, and can truly make a difference, be it in your life, someone else's, or both.

# *Meditation for Intention*

1. Sit somewhere quiet.

2. Close your eyes.

3. Be aware of any sounds, thoughts, feelings or sensations in your body. Simply observe them.

4. Put your focus and awareness onto your breath.

5. Take a few deep breaths in and out.

6. Say silently, "What is my intention for today?"

7. Say silently, "Let my intention be motivated from my higher self."

8. Say silently, "I am ready to set my intention."

9. Say silently, "My intention for today is (fill in what you want that to be)."

10. When you are ready, bring your focus and awareness back to your body.

11. Slowly open your eyes.

12. *When you are ready, transition out of your meditation.*

## Note to self:

*I begin each day with a clear intention*
*May my intention create the best results*
*May others benefit from my intentions*

# CHAPTER 25

# Service

*We are all here on earth to help others; what on earth*
*the others are here for I don't know.*
—W. H. Auden

Have you ever forgotten something important, like someone's birthday, or anniversary? Or told someone you would do something, and you forgot? Maybe you haven't talked to someone that you care about in a while because you've been too busy to reach out.

We've all experienced either being too busy or forgetful about something that involved someone else, or had it done to us, and when it's happened, we felt bad. It's not that we intended to do something that could hurt someone's feel-

223

ings, but sometimes we can be in that "me-centric" bubble I talked about in the Chapter 22 (Compassion), and "If you're walking around in it, there is so much you miss."

Where Mindfulness comes into play here is that when we're present, and more aware in a moment, we're less likely to be forgetful, or not think of others. Even if we're busy, we make that extra effort to find time to show someone we care about them, and not just make what we're doing, or what's happening in our life more important than them. It's as if Mindfulness stretches our bandwidth to include other people in our thoughts, even when we're busy, and reminds us again and again not to just think of ourselves. Again, remember what I said in the chapter on Compassion, "Mindfulness will always keep you on the compassion track. When you're present, and your awareness is heightened, you can't but be aware of others", and by being more mindful, it inspires us to think of ways we can give of ourselves to lift someone's spirits, and make them happy.

The saying, "Tis better to give than to receive" is true, but maybe not for everyone. There are plenty of people who would invert that quote and say it is much better to receive. But you now know my thoughts on inverting something to what it wasn't intended for. You're messing with the truth. And when you do that, you're not living your higher self at all. It's like you've made a conscious decision to go for the lowest hanging fruit because it's more convenient for you, and as you devour it, you could care less about sharing it with anyone else.

There is no doubt that when you give, you receive, and what you receive can be so much more than what you thought you would. But you have to be willing to not put yourself before others, which might not be so easy for you to do.

It's hard to admit what we might not be so proud of about ourselves. Maybe we put ourselves first because we were neglected as a child, or we come from nothing, and have had to fight for everything we have. Maybe it's because we have felt so unloved our whole life, that putting someone before us can feel like they will get the love we desperately need, and there will be nothing left for us. There are many reasons why we put ourselves first before another, but when we make the decision to put someone before us, we can feel that we have extra to give, and that feeling only expands, the more generous we are.

Being in service to others is one of the most gratifying things we can do. There's a great Chinese proverb that goes: "If you want happiness for an hour, take a nap. If you want happiness for a day, go fishing. If you want happiness for a year, inherit a fortune. If you want happiness for a lifetime, help somebody." Living our lives only serving our needs means you're living your life always satisfying your immediate desires, which I spoke about in Chapter 13 (Desire).

Remember what Buddha said: "Desire causes suffering because of our constant need for it." When you are in service to others, you do it from a genuine place of already being satisfied, and don't feel that you have to be constantly feeding your own needs for more satisfaction. He who serves is abundant, and will always feel that they have more than they need to satisfy themselves.

At one point in our lives, we're going to have to accept that we're not put on this earth just to take care of our own needs.

And even though we can be very divided in what that means, and we see that divide politically between the "haves and have nots", we may feel that "what's mine is mine, and what's yours is yours" or, as some people feel, "what's mine is mine, and what's yours is mine." Hopefully, you will realize that what is yours may be yours, but that doesn't mean you're entitled to more than others, or what you have can't be shared, especially with those that have less than you, or maybe even nothing.

At some point, whether it's of your own choosing, or it is being asked of you, you will be called to step up to serve someone—an aging relative, a child, a neighbor in need—and have to make a decision that will determine who you really are, and what you're made of. If you think you're above what is essentially asked of all of us, think again. Each of us will be called to give, or to "serve somebody", and whether we do, or we don't, we will have to live with that decision. Or, in Shakespeare's words, "To thine own self be true."

I almost prefer our more modern version of Shakespeare, Bob Dylan, whose lyrics in "Gotta Serve Somebody" say it all: *"Still, you're gonna have to serve somebody, yes you're gonna have to serve somebody."*

So, as the lyrics continue, whether you're an "ambassador," or a "construction worker" or you "wear cotton" or "wear silk", think about how you can give, and how you can serve another. And know that when you do, you will feel so much more than your identity, or role, or persona, or whatever you think defines you.

The most important thing that will define you is how you lived your life. Did you give, or did you take? Were you compassionate, or indifferent? If you want to know the answer to that, ask yourself, "Who am I?"

If you still can't find the answer, think of what Gandhi said: "The best way to find yourself is to lose yourself in the service of others."

# Meditation for Service

1. Sit somewhere quiet.

2. Close your eyes.

3. Be aware of any sounds, thoughts, feelings or sensations you may have in your body. Simply observe them.

4. Put your focus and awareness onto your breath.

5. Take a few deep breaths in and out.

6. Say silently, "How can I be in service?"

7. Say silently, "Whom can I serve?"

8. Say silently, "I am ready to serve."

9. When you're ready, bring your focus and awareness back to your body.

10. Slowly open your eyes.

11. *When you are ready, transition out of your meditation.*

*Note to self:*

*It pleases me to give to others*
*I am open to being in service*
*How can I best serve?*

# PART IV

## Realization

*With realization of one's own potential and self-confidence in one's ability, one can build a better world.*
*—Dalai Lama*

*Once the realization is accepted that even between the closest human beings, infinite distances continue, a wonderful living side by side can grow, if they succeed in loving the distance between them which makes it possible for each to see the other whole against the sky.*
*—Rainer Maria Rilke*

## CHAPTER 26

# Reality

*Reality exists in the human mind, and nowhere else.*
*—George Orwell*

*There is no reality except the one contained within us.*
*That is why so many people live such an unreal life.*
*They take the images outside of them for reality and*
*never allow the world within to assert itself.*
*—Hermann Hesse*

Reality is defined as "The state of things as they actually exist." But what I think exists and what you think exists might not be the same thing.  So, does that mean we have a different perception of reality?  I think that's obviously very true, so how do we live in a world with different perceptions of reality, successfully? God knows we're trying, and how successful we are at it will be determined by what ultimately happens in my, yours, or our reality, depending on how you look at it.

But in this very moment of "now", why don't we hold the thought that reality is beautiful, and hope that by holding that thought, we can create a reality we agree on. By doing so, it can become the very thing we believe is possible.

Wouldn't it be great if we could create a universal reality like that? Just hold the same lovely thought in our minds, with the same intention, and the world would reflect back to us exactly what we wished for.

If we believe that our thoughts create our reality, then it is mirroring back to us what we've wished for, or held as our intention. But clearly our intentions differ, and what the world shows us is how extremely different our intentions are. In the macro/microcosm I spoke about in Chapter 22 (Compassion), I said, "Think of how you can leave your house today, and what it is you want to take out into your world because your world, in your city, in your life, in your mini universe, represents the entire world, and so is the same with everyone in their mini universes."

Reality will always reflect back to us where we are in our consciousness.

To the degree that we are awake, so will reality mirror that back to us. If we see that in our "mini universe" things aren't working, then we know that something is wrong, and the steps we need to take to be more awake and aware, which is practicing Mindfulness daily, we are not taking.

Remember, if we begin each day setting our intention with total awareness, and are completely clear about what it is we want to manifest, and why, then we are doing what we need to on our end to create a better reality, not just for ourselves, but everybody.

The reason is we are part of what is called the "collective unconscious," a term coined by Carl Jung, which means that there is "an unconscious mind that is shared by all of humanity." This is different than the "collective consciousness" I spoke about, which are things we share and are commonly understood, like, our "beliefs, ideas and moral attitudes." What is unconscious, or not known to us, is what lies beneath the surface in each of us. Perhaps it's not spoken about, or shared, or maybe even hidden, not just from others, but also ourselves.

What that means to me is that my work, even before I set my intention, is to make sure that whatever is not known to me, or what I am unaware of about myself, is made conscious to me, which means, I wake up even more to who I really am. That also means I have to shine a light on my "shadow"; the darker, or unlikable aspects of myself I may or may not be aware of, which I spoke about in Chapter 15 (Knowledge). I asked, "What is it that we have still to learn? That we are afraid to know ourselves, and fearful of what we may find out? That there is darkness there?" and I answered, "Of course there is darkness there. There is darkness in everyone, and it is called the 'shadow,' and if we don't make it conscious to us, it will, Jung said, 'appear in our lives as fate.' "

If we want to go straight to the direct source of our reality, all we need to know is how much light have we shined on ourselves to find out if we haven't cleared up any remnants of our own darkness, which is only confusion caused by the absence of light. If you haven't, you can be assured that it will play a role in your current reality, which by the way, changes constantly depending on where we are in our consciousness. From a Buddhist perspective, "we have a constantly changing steam of consciousness," which I interpret as my consciousness changes as I do.

I know, you thought all you had to do was set your intentions, and *voila*, the perfect reality will appear. Well, not so fast. I mean, if you feel you've done all of the prerequisites it takes to create the perfect reality you see fit for yourself, then, yes, a perfect reality may very well appear for you.

But the thing to remember about our "awakening" is that it's a daily process. Just like how our car's windshield gets dirty each day, and we use our windshield wipers to clean it, you too have to do a thorough sweep of yourself to find out what's dirtying or obstructing your reality. You may think everything is a "go" in the reality department, but unless you're committed to being fully present in each and every moment of your life, and awake as you possibly can be, then your reality will mirror back to you what isn't working. Maybe you're not as awake as you think you are, but hopefully you'll be aware of that too. As Russian esotericist P.D. Ouspensky said, "When one realizes one is asleep, at that moment one is already half-awake."

So, reality is determined by how awake we are, unless we think that this is all a dream, which it may very well be.

But even if this is a dream, wouldn't we want to experience it with total awareness, or else we will be experiencing absolutely nothing, and that, to me, means we no longer exist.

What does reality mean to you? Is it something you feel you are creating, or do you feel it is being created for you? Do you think your reality is pre-destined, or do you think you are creating your destiny? Maybe you don't give much thought to these types of questions, and like I said about consciousness, "As elusive or mysterious as consciousness can be, we still can decide how we want to live it, depending on what it personally means to us." Nobody can tell us what consciousness is, because it's different for each and every person. As I said, it could mean something spiritual, or scientific, or abstract, or absolutely nothing to you. That's right, consciousness can mean "nothing." And maybe you feel the same way about reality. But whatever it means to you, you should know that you have a very important role in creating your reality, and even if it isn't going exactly as you want it to go, today could be the very day that it changes.

So, what do you want your reality to be today, right this very moment? Let's start with that. What do you see creating for yourself? You can make it as elaborate or as over the top as you want, but remember, what you hold in your mind's eye becomes your reality.

As Buddha said:

*Keep your thoughts positive,*
*Because your thoughts become your words.*
*Keep your words positive,*
*Because your words become your behaviors.*

*Keep your behaviors positive,*
*Because your behaviors become your habits,*
*Keep your habits positive,*
*Because your habits become your values,*
*Keep your values positive,*
*Because your values become your destiny.*

# Meditation for Reality

1. Sit somewhere quiet.

2. Gently close your eyes.

3. Be aware of any sounds, thoughts, feelings or sensations you may be feeling in your body. Simply observe them.

4. Put your focus and awareness onto your breath.

5. Say silently, "What is my reality?"

6. Say silently, "What reality do I wish to create?"

7. Say silently, "Today I choose to create a better reality."

8. Say silently, "May my reality be filled with light and love for myself and others."

9. When you are ready, bring your focus and awareness back to your body.

10. Slowly open your eyes.

11. *Take the time you need to transition out of your meditation.*

## *Note to self:*

*My thoughts create my reality*
*I choose positive thoughts to create my reality*
*I am creating the reality I want*

## CHAPTER 27

# Destiny

*It is not in the stars to hold our destiny but in ourselves.*
—*Shakespeare*

If you were asked before you were born what would you want your destiny to be, what would you have answered? Would you have wanted it to be different than it has been so far, or the same? Would you have wanted to be doing the same work, or have the same job? Would you have wanted to live where you are? Would you have wanted the same family and friends to be on your life journey with you? Would you have wanted to be someone other than yourself?

Now ask yourself those questions as if today is the beginning of your destiny. What can you do differently? Do you want to keep your job, or go after the job of your dreams? Do you want to live where you are, or move to somewhere so remote and foreign, it's only a place you read and swoon about in travel magazines? Do you want the same family and friends to continue on your life journey with you, or are you ready to move on from the ones you've grown apart from? Do you want to be different than who you are right now, or do you secretly want to reinvent yourself and be the new you?

The absolute magnificence of being who we are in the present is that it really can be different than any other time before it, and will be different than any other time after it, so right now is when we can decide how we want our destiny to unfold from this moment onward. It's like constantly having a new beginning. Isn't that exciting?

Mindfulness is the most freeing way to live because you get to be in the moment not bound to anything other than just being present and aware.

You get to experience an expansiveness that feels like you're breathing along with all of nature around you, which is like the sky is breathing with you, and the trees are breathing with you, and the birds are breathing with you. There is no feeling of separateness. Like I described in Chapter 7 (Wholeness): "Many people who meditate say they experience that feeling when they sit quietly, and can feel as if they are no longer just a person (self) sitting in meditation, but rather selfless, and connected to something that is everything." Isn't that how you want to feel as you continue on your destiny? To feel connected to everything in such a way that you can meet each moment as your most authentic self, and know that you are designing your destiny exactly as you choose to?

Everything fades away into the background when we live our lives focused on that one thing that is most real. That could be gazing into someone's eyes, and seeing the beauty of their soul, or holding a baby, and feeling a newborn's life in our arms, or looking up at the sky, realizing how life is as temporary as a cloud moving across it. Whatever it is we choose to focus on with awareness, it reminds us that our destiny is filled with all of the moments we are experiencing. So, what do we want the moments of our destiny to be from this moment onward?

You can either continue on the path of your destiny, as you have been living it up to now, or you can completely change the course of it by deciding that you want it to be different starting now.

Some people believe that their destiny has been decided for them, and their lives are "pre-destined", or as I said Chapter 26 (Reality), "Maybe you feel that you are creating your destiny."

Whatever you may feel about it, ask yourself how you would create it, whether you think you are, or someone or something else is doing it for you. If you are, in fact, the great "creator" of your destiny in your "mini universe" what would that be? You certainly can imagine it, and hold a vision in your mind's eye. And as you hold that vision, ask yourself that most important question of all questions; "Who am I?"

In your answer lies the compass for your destiny. It will tell you where you must go on the path of self-realization.

It will give you directions, and even if they seem unclear, or cryptic, or even mysterious, it will become more clear, as you become more aware. And when you become more aware, you can trust that you have your destiny map right there in the wholeness of your being, and you can follow it always. And if, or when, you feel that you have gone off course, which you will because as you know by now, you are having a "human experience" and may lose sight of your "spiritual being" again and again along the way.

But when you stop and breathe, and remember that you are present in this moment, right here, right now, you can call upon your higher self, your "spiritual being" to be the navigator of the ship on this great, vast ocean of life that you are sailing on. And as you move along on it, you will know with certainty that your most knowing, wise, divine, higher-self desires one thing, and one thing only: to live this life as it was meant for you, and no one else.

Sail away on this great cosmic journey. You are getting that much closer to the *land of oneness*, because you are taking yourself closer to it by choosing to live authentically as who you truly are. I hope to see you there, and together we can live as "one". You and I, and all that exists, oh, and yes, divine cosmos, you will know yourself even better once we arrive.

# *Meditation for Destiny*

1. Sit somewhere quiet.

2. Close your eyes.

3. Be aware of any sounds, thoughts, feelings or sensations in your body. Simply observe them.

4. Say silently, "I am creating my destiny."

5. Say silently, "I am ready to meet it."

6. Repeat as many times as you wish.

7. When you are ready, bring your focus and awareness back to your body.

8. Slowly open your eyes.

9. *When you are ready, transition out of your meditation.*

*Note to self:*

*Hello destiny*
*Let's set sail!*

CHAPTER 28

# Self-Realization

*Your own Self-Realization is the greatest service*
*you can render the world.*
—*Ramana Maharshi*

D o you remember that famous scene in the movie *Rocky*,
when he ran up seventy-two steps to the top of the
Philadelphia Museum, and once he got there he raised his
arms triumphantly? He had met his challenge as a small-
time boxer to become a heavyweight champion, which was
something he believed he could be. That's you on the path
of self-realization. You're a champ on this life journey, yet
it's no easy road getting to the top step where you can raise
your arms victoriously, and declare, "I made it!"

But here's what you should know about yourself. You've walked a lot farther than 72 steps—way farther. And along the way, you've tripped, and fell, and maybe even rolled down them, and hurt yourself pretty badly. And maybe you looked up at the steps of your life journey, and said, "No way, I'm not taking one more step. I'm done, I'm through!" But you picked yourself up, dusted yourself off, and began again, one step at a time.

And that is the path of self-realization. We "begin again" each time we get knocked down along the way, and get up because we are determined to realize our full potential.

We do it because we believe in ourselves, and even when we don't, there is something greater in us that pushes us forward, and tells us to continue on. It's an arduous journey to become self-realized, which is like sailing on the vast, tempestuous ocean to meet our destiny. The sea will rage along the way, and toss our boat around, but we will be tested to see if we have what it takes to keep going. And if we don't give up, we will meet our potential, and can triumphantly raise our arms in the air like Rocky and declare, "I made it!"

So, do you have what it takes to keep going, and make it today, in this moment? Self-realization is like running a marathon, not just once, but again and again, as many times as possible so that each time you realize more of your potential, and you keep on going. It's not because you have to get to the finish line, but that you're doing it to realize more of who you are—your higher self, your "spiritual being". You understand that the marathon—the journey of self-realization—is never ending.

That's why the quote, "It's not the destination, but the journey," is so resonant. Because it's true. It is the journey that teaches us who we are, and that means every step of our journey.

We may be hurried or impatient to get to our "destination" but once we're there, what is it that we think we will find? We will find ourselves, and that means whatever "realizations" we've had along the way. Each of those realizations are like mini awakenings. On the path of self-realization, there is no one big awakening, but many along the way of varying degrees: some small, some big; and each one of them is like the lotus flower, which grows out of muddy waters. Our hard work on the path of self-realization is like the journey of the lotus flower. It's the challenges and the difficulties that we face along the way that is similar to the mud the lotus must emerge from, and it is the light that we shine on ourselves that opens us up to our full potential, just like the lotus flower opens to the sun of a new day.

And it is a new day. It is the day of "now," and no other day has come before it that is like this one.

You have awakened to this day to become more self-realized, and you will emerge from whatever this day presents to you triumphantly, but as I said in Chapter 20 (Honesty), "Each day we have some type of honesty test that we face."

So be honest with yourself in whatever it is you face, and even if you feel that you can't take one more step on your life journey, take it anyway because you can. Remember, Goethe said, "Magic is believing in yourself, if you can do that, you can make anything happen."

But know that self-realization is the ultimate inside job, and anyone who has the belief, strength, stamina, and sheer determination to become who they really are, and be willing to strip away every single peace of false clothing, which is much more than what we wear, but the layers upon layers of the artificial, inauthentic self, and the illusionary thoughts that fill our minds, only then will the egg of illusion crack open. What will be born is who you were when you came into existence; an already enlightened being.

I believe that self-realization is a rebirth of one's true self. And we can be reborn again and again. So, whether you're reborn in this incarnation, or another one, if you believe in the afterlife, time will tell, and as we know about time, it continues on.

So, don't be concerned about "when" you will become self-realized. Just stay on this path of awakening, and be on it because you genuinely want to realize your true self, and not live your life falsely as someone you're not. That, in itself, is a realization, and on the life journey, the more realizations you have, the closer you will get to your full potential. That is what will motivate you to continue on, no matter how many more marathons there are to run, or steps to run up, or how many more times the waters rage as you continue sailing upon the vast sea of your destiny.

# Meditation for Self-Realization

1. Sit somewhere quiet.

2. Gently close your eyes.

3. Be aware of any sounds, thoughts, feelings or sensations in your body. Simply observe them.

4. Put your focus and attention onto your breath.

5. Take a few deep breaths in and out.

6. Say silently, "Self-realization is my path."

7. Say silently, "I am committed to the path of awakening."

8. Say silently, "May I fulfill my potential."

9. Bring your focus and awareness back to your body.

10. Slowly open your eyes.

11. *When you are ready, transition out of your meditation.*

*Note to self:*

*I am committed to stripping away the layers
of my false self
I desire to realize my true self
I am unafraid to meet who I really am
I am ready to live my full potential*

# CHAPTER 29

# I Am

*I am not afraid... I was born to do this.*
*—Joan of Arc*

"I am that I am." This is one of the most famous verses in the Torah, when Moses asked God his name. Is that an answer each one of us can give when asked who we are, and if so, who is it that we are?

There have been many implications as to what God's answer means, and it has been translated to the future tense in English Bibles, "I am what I will be" or "shall be." That, for me, means, we are in the process of becoming who we are, and depending on what we allow ourselves to be, or aspire to be, the answer will reflect exactly who we are today.

Which brings us back again to Mindfulness. Who we are in this very moment is who we are right now, just as God was who he was when Moses asked him his name. And the answer, "I am that I am," can be said at any moment of our lives. When we ask ourselves, "Who am I?" we will face who we are in the moment, and who that is can either be who we want to be, or not.

But there comes a time when we must declare who we are, and stand by it, even if it isn't who we are yet.

The words "I am" are powerful. We are declaring who we are to the universe. So, what is it that we want to announce? On the path of self-realization, we strive to meet our full potential, and live true to who we really are. We know this is an ongoing journey, but if we stand tall and proud, and say, "This is who I am today, right now, in this moment" then that becomes our truth. A decision has been made, and it has been said, and whether we declare it to the universe, or say it silently to ourselves, we know that we are ready to meet our greater self on the path of self-realization.

So, then; who are you? Can you answer that and stand tall and proud as you say it?

Don't judge yourself. That is not what this question asks of you.

It asks you to dig deep into your heart and soul, and reach even deeper into the sacred room of your house of self, and find your most true self there. That is where you can speak from and answer proudly, "I am that I am!" If so, who is it that you are? Have you stripped away your false selves, the layers that are not you, and the illusionary thoughts that occupy your mind that tell you what isn't true? Have you plunged into your being to find out who you really are, which I spoke about in Chapter 10 (Self), "by scuba-diving to the bottom of the deep blue sea of your psyche," you discovered "some wreckage there, and maybe remnants of a sunken ship," but you also found treasures there too, and "the deeper you go, the more treasures you may find, and they can be the most beautiful things you've ever seen."

Who you are is all of that. You are the pain that you've suffered, and you are the treasures you have found from your pain. You are the mud, and you are the lotus. You are self-realized, and you are more potential you have not yet fulfilled.

We are becoming our "I am" every single moment of our lives. Be the best "I am" that you can be right now, this very moment, and if anyone asks you who you are, say with confidence, "I am that I am!" Who that is, is who they will see you as, just as Moses saw God. They will see who you are, and they will know your name, and you will be known for who it is that you truly are. And that will carry you beyond the present, and into all of the days of your life.

# Meditation for "I am"

1. Sit somewhere quiet.

2. Close your eyes gently.

3. Be aware of any sounds, thoughts, feelings or sensations in your body. Simply observe them.

4. Put your focus and awareness onto your breath.

5. Take a few deep breaths in and out.

6. Say silently, "I am."

7. Say silently, "I am that I am."

8. Say silently, "See me as I am."

9. When you are ready bring your focus and awareness back to your body.

10. Slowly open your eyes.

11. *When you are ready, transition out of your meditation.*

## Note to self:

*I am that I am*
*I am me*
*I am you*
*We are one*

# CHAPTER 30

# Oneness

*I am he*
*As you are he*
*As you are me*
*And we are all together.*
*—The Beatles, "I am the Walrus"*

*All differences in this world are of degree, and not of*
*kind, because oneness is the secret of everything.*
*—Swami Vivekananda*

Congratulations, you have arrived to the *land of oneness*! Yes, you are here, and as you look around, you see that you didn't need to go anywhere to get here. No plane, no train, or automobile. Not a single suitcase needed to be packed. Although everything looks the same, something seems different. Very different. You feel yourself connected to everything and everyone, and you have this feeling in your heart like it's as wide as the world, and it is.

The land of oneness lives in your heart, and has been waiting for you to return to it for a very long time.

It was patient, and unconditional in its love for you, and knew that you had many steps to walk, many marathons to run, and a long, difficult voyage on the vast sea of your destiny before you got here, and you did. Go ahead, raise your arms up in the air like Rocky did, and say triumphantly, "I made it!"

You probably have this feeling that you've been here before, and you have. You were born here. This is your birthplace, and everyone else's birthplace. This land of oneness is everyone's land, and even though we live on a great big planet, thousands and thousands of miles apart, the land of oneness is where we will return to, when we are ready to live together as one. But we don't need to travel to be together because everyone has the land of oneness in their heart, just like you do, and all you can hope for is that they discover it too.

But many people won't because they are very disconnected from their heart, as I spoke about in Chapter 17 (Love), because they fear it.

And that's what's really going on.

There is so much fear around love that people can't live successfully no matter what land they live in, and the land of oneness is so foreign to them, you may as well be speaking about Mars. If you said to someone who is not connected to their heart, "Do you know you have a place inside your heart, and it's called the land of oneness?" they'll probably look at you like you're weird or crazy, and think you're one of those peace and love kind of hippies or a new age person that's so out of touch with reality, they can't take you seriously.

But going back to George Orwell's quote at the top of Chapter 26 (Reality), "Reality exists in the human mind, and nowhere else." That means that we all have different realities from one another, and if you know that living in oneness is the truest reality of all, then you're going to have to be honest and brave, and continue living your life knowing the greatest truth of all: *we are one.*

Sometimes I think the cosmos is laughing at us because we're so out of touch with what's really going on. If we go with Carl Sagan's theory that it's learning from us, it's probably shaking its billion stars head, and thinking, "Come on already, figure this thing out, and stop endangering yourselves and the planet!"

In the land of oneness love is the religion, and everyone practices it. No one really cares how you dress, or what gender you are, or what work you do, or what car you drive, or where you live, because everyone knows they share the same belief, and that is "Love is all there is." And they're kind and compassionate to one another, and everyone lets you go in front of them in traffic, and not only hold the door open for you, but they ask you how you are, and tell you how nice you look, and put their arm around you like a child, and say, "I like you, and want you to be my friend." I know that sounds mushy and unrealistic, but if we don't bring some more kindness to how we treat one another, the world will continue to function more and more unkindly, and we will get ourselves into more and more trouble with one another. Who knows what's going to happen.

Our climate is changing, our poverty is growing, our politics are dividing us, our religions are separating us. No matter what side of oneness you are on, something has to change, and that means in present time, right now, right here. ***Today!***

That brings it back to you and Mindfulness. Be present every single moment of your life as your most truthful and authentic self, meaning that you are awake and aware in each one of them. And if, or when, you slip out of a moment, which you will, because that can happen in the land of oneness too, as it can even in paradise; we can forget who we are. Hmm, I think that's what got us into trouble in the first place if you want to get biblical about it, and view the land of oneness as the Garden of Eden.  But that story has been written, rewritten, revised, re-revised and co-opted so many times that we've lost the plot and its meaning.

So now it's time for us to write our own story. What do we want that story to tell, and how do we want the story to end?

You decide. You are the author, but you are much more than that. You are the teacher, the leader, the guru, and the creator of all that lives in your reality. So, what do you want that reality to be?

Moses asked God his name, and he answered; I am that I am." Who are you?

We will know each other by our name, and our name will be who we are. Not our identity, not our role, not our persona, not our title, not our race, not our religion, not any of that. Who we are is how we lived our truth, and how we lived that truth is what **shall remain.**

I hope to meet you in the land of oneness. I look forward to spending time with you there, my friend, and together we can live in peace and in love.

# Meditation for Oneness

1. Sit somewhere quiet.

2. Close your eyes gently.

3. Put your focus and awareness onto your breath.

4. Take a few deep breaths in and out.

5. Say silently, "Oneness."

6. Repeat as many times as you wish.

7. Bring your focus and awareness back to your breath.

8. Slowly open your eyes.

9. *When you're ready, transition out of your meditation.*

*Note to self:*

**Oneness**

# ABOUT THE AUTHOR

**O**ra **Nadrich** is the Founder and President of The Institute For Transformational Thinking. She is a Life Coach, Thought Coach, Mindfulness Meditation teacher, and author of *Says Who? How One Simple Question Can Change The Way You Think Forever.*

Ora's extensive psycho-spiritual exploration in Jungian Analysis, Buddhism, Cognitive Behavioral Therapy (CBT), Technology of Change, and Kabbalah has influenced her work. Ora is a frequent blogger for the Huffington Post, and has been featured as a panelist on Huffington Post Live. She's written many articles on Mindfulness for Yahoo

Health, Women's Health, Success Magazine, Spirituality & Health, MindBodyGreen, and many other publications. She leads workshops on Transformational Thinking and The Says Who? Method; a step-by-step process of confronting our negative thoughts, which are what often create the obstacles in our lives. Providing both tangible and practical lessons, Ora's students are able to address and overcome their negative thoughts and outlooks to live their lives at their highest potential. Among her other workshops are *Mindfulness Matters, Living a Mindful Life, Conscious Manifestation,* and *Love, Sex, & Mindfulness.*

Ora was an actress and screenwriter, where she worked in film, episodic television, and commercials for more than a decade, which she feels provided her vast experience in exploring motivation and the process of self-discovery. During that time, she simultaneously embarked on a two-decade psychological and spiritual journey toward self-awareness and transformation, which lead her to becoming a Life Coach. She currently offers Thought Coach Certification Trainings through her educational organization, The IFTT.

Ora lives in Los Angeles with her husband, Jeff, and two sons, Jake and Benjamin.

CPSIA information can be obtained
at www.ICGtesting.com
Printed in the USA
LVHW052054150919
631103LV00005B/68/P

9 780578 432106